ISRAEL

THE WILL TO PREVAIL

DANNY DANON

palgrave
macmillan

First published in 2012 by PALGRAVE MACMILLAN® in the U.S.—a
division of St. Martin's Press LLC, 175 Fifth Avenue, New York, NY
10010.

Where this book is distributed in the UK, Europe, and the rest of
the world, this is by Palgrave Macmillan, a division of Macmillan
Publishers Limited, registered in England, company number 785998,
of Houndmills, Basingstoke, Hampshire RG21 6XS.

Palgrave Macmillan is the global academic imprint of the above
companies and has companies and representatives throughout the
world.

Palgrave® and Macmillan® are registered trademarks in the United
States, the United Kingdom, Europe, and other countries.

ISBN: 978-0-230-34176-0

Library of Congress Cataloging-in-Publication Data
Danon, Danny.
    Israel : the will to prevail / Danny Danon.
        p.   cm.
    ISBN 978-0-230-34176-0
    1. Arab-Israeli conflict. 2. Arab-Israeli conflict.—Causes. 3. Arab-
Israeli conflict.—Influence. 4. Arab-Israeli conflict—1993—Peace.
5. Middle East—Foreign relations—Israel. 6. Israel—Foreign
relations—Middle East. 7. Israel—History. I. Title.
    DS119.7.D2574 2012
    956.05'3—dc23

                                                         2012010454

A catalogue record of the book is available from the British Library.

Design by Letra Libre, Inc.

First edition: September 2012

10 9 8 7 6 5 4 3 2 1

Printed in the United States of America.

*This book is dedicated to the memory of
my late father, Joseph Danon, a genuine
Israeli patriot who fought all his life.*

CONTENTS

ACKNOWLEDGMENTS

THERE ARE SO MANY PEOPLE WHOM I WISH TO THANK FOR helping me to complete my first book. As someone who values the importance of heritage, I would like to start with my father, Joseph Danon, to whom I also dedicate the book. Even though the time I spent with my father was limited, I am grateful for the unique period with him, which shaped my personality. I want to thank him from the day I was born until the day he passed away for the seed he planted within me that cultivated my involvement with Israel's future and gave me the strength and courage to stand behind my principles.

My dad chose to name me after Daniel Vardon, his legendary commander in the reconnaissance special unit. Daniel Vardon was, for my father, the symbol of the ultimate Zionist hero. Daniel Vardon was born in 1939 in Kibbutz Givat Brenner. He was a leader in his community, and during his military service he received two of the highest distinctions for his heroic actions during two operations on the Syrian border. On the third day of the Six-Day War, he headed his troops of the reconnaissance special unit into the Egyptian city El Arish. Daniel Vardon risked his life in a heroic rescue operation again. After hearing the reports about a unit of his soldiers that was wounded and trapped in a small alley, where an Egyptian sniper was located in a strategic location and shot anyone who tried to get closer to the wounded Israeli soldiers, Daniel Vardon did not hesitate and tried to lead a rescue operation. This was his last heroic decision; he was shot dead by the sniper. The loss of his beloved commander was a hard moment for my father, who fought with his admired commander in this special unit and spent days and nights navigating and exploring the land with him.

Only two years later my father was severely wounded during an army operation in the Jorday Valley. Despite his complete hearing loss and severe head wounds, which dragged him to hospitals on a regular basis, my father was very knowledgeable and had a genuine and informal love of the land and people of Israel. He was able to teach me the history of our nation, and, in his unique way, he encouraged me to get involved and to not be afraid to stand behind my ideas. As a child who received his Jewish and Zionist education mostly from hearing the stories of my father and reading books, I learned to appreciate the importance of words, whether spoken or written.

Special thanks to my beloved mother, Jocheved Danon, a real "Eshet Chayl"—a woman of valor who, despite the complex situation she found herself at a very young age, gathered enormous inner strength to provide our family with a warm and caring home. With her unique and quiet intelligence, she provided me with the self-confidence to stick to my beliefs and principles. As someone who was born before the establishment of the State of Israel and who experienced in childhood the feeling of the siege on Jerusalem during the War of Independence, she always stressed the importance of controlling your own destiny. I am deeply grateful for everything she gave me and admire her decision to dedicate her life to her husband day and night, to commemorate his memory, and to be there for her grandchildren: Ela, Rotem, Maya, Aviad, Yonathan, Hila, Daniel, Shira, and Tomie.

To my beloved wife, Talie, thank you very much for being there; I know that when I am not at home, you are there for our children and I am grateful for it. Without your encouragement and support I would not have been able to complete this book. Thank you for being so special, smart, and funny, and especially thank you for allowing me to fulfill my dreams and passions.

To my children: Aviad, Hila, and Shira, who inspire me every single day with their happiness and optimism. I wish you all the joy and happiness there is. I shall always give you all the love I have.

To my brother Eyal and my sister Shirly, who patiently listened to all my stories during our childhood, I am sure that our dad would have been very proud of you, your wonderful spouses, Ely and Odelia, and especially would have great pride in his grand-children whom he was not able to meet.

Special thanks and love for my parents-in-law, Shalom and Dina, for your unconditional support. Hearing Shalom's singing on Friday nights in our synagogue really gives inspiration and strengthens one's belief.

Writing a book like this does not happen in a vacuum. I would like to thank Dr. Jonathan Spyer for his advice. Thanks also go to Mitchell Bard of the Jewish Virtual Library for his invaluable in-sights and information into many aspects of Israeli history and the position in which Israel often finds itself on American college cam-puses. Dr. Rafael Medof, director of the David S. Wyman Institute for Holocaust Studies, also shared important background material on World War II and the Holocaust. Salomon Benzimra, cofounder of Canadians for Israel's Legal Rights, provided valuable background and perspective on Balfour, the San Remo Conference, and the founding of the State of Israel. I also want to thank Carol Mann, my literary agent, for her wisdom and experience. Many thanks to Karen Wolny and to the great team at Palgrave Macmillan for all their support. Last but not least, I would like to deeply thank Karen Kelly, who worked tirelessly with me on this book. Thank you very much, Karen, for your amazing patience and support.

INTRODUCTION

STANDING ON A PRECIPICE

I REPRESENT A NEW GENERATION OF LEADERS WHO SEE Israel taking a different and more autonomous path than it has over the past several decades. In many ways, our outlook echoes that of the founding generation, who understood that we may have to engage, albeit reluctantly, in armed conflict to secure a Jewish state. I've lived through years of terrorism and war and have seen the toll they have taken on my own family and on my neighbors, friends, and colleagues. As deputy speaker of the Knesset, my goal is to protect the people I serve and the land I love. In both roles, citizen and public servant, I'm fully cognizant of the dangers threatening our society. But I also see a tremendous opportunity for Israel to realize a vision of lasting peace and stability for its people and the region, one we must take advantage of *now*.

Throughout its history, Israel has conducted its affairs with the aim of pleasing—or at least not offending—its strongest partner and closest ally: the United States. American support for our fragile and fledgling nation has been crucial to our success as a nation, and for that, all Israelis are blessed and eternally grateful. However, history shows that when we act on our own, according to our own best interests, the results are better not only for Israel, but for world peace as a whole.

We are now at a critical juncture in our brief but momentous history, and our very survival is once again at stake. This is also a watershed moment for U.S.-Israeli relations. The Obama administration has sent mixed signals to the Arab world. On the one hand, the president left troops in Iraq and Afghanistan longer than was initially expected. The administration has also killed several terrorists, many of whom are seen as heroes in the Middle East, including Osama bin Laden, acts that I applaud. On the other hand, Obama's Cairo speech extended an olive branch further than previous presidents had done. Moreover, the Obama administration support for the Palestinian position and their engagement of the Muslim Brotherhood in Egypt call the strength of its support for Israel into question. For example, as a consequence, many Palestinian leaders believe they can achieve statehood now without granting any concessions.

Even the little-reported reversal of Secretary of State Hillary Clinton's position on Jerusalem as the capital of Israel, which contradicts her statements as New York's junior senator, is a startling reminder of the growing rift between the United States and Israel. In a brief filed with the Supreme Court in September,[1] she wrote that any American action, even symbolically, toward recognizing Jerusalem as the capital of Israel must be avoided because it might jeopardize the peace process. She may be following the president's lead on this, because she is carrying out his wishes on foreign policy. I can only speculate as to her motivations, but the formal move indicates a strategic reassessment going on in Washington today that may well end by downgrading the importance of Israel in U.S. policy.

Indeed a U.S. jurist has also sent such mixed signals, showing that the U.S. political left wing feels particularly comfortable advising those who may not have our best interests at heart. In an Egyptian interview with President Clinton–appointed U.S. Supreme Court justice Ruth Bader Ginsburg, which aired on Al-Hayat TV on January 30, 2012, she advised the new Muslim Brotherhood government, "You should certainly be aided by all the constitution-writing that has gone on since the end of World War II. I would not look to the U.S. constitution, if I were drafting a constitution in the year 2012. I might look at the constitution of South Africa."[2] This may seem benign to some, but to me such advice reads as a trivialization and disregard for a document Judge Ginsburg has sworn to protect. What message does this send to those listening? Ultimately, it can be read as U.S. weakness by those in the Middle East.

Many in the region interpret the growing irrelevance of U.S. policy, in the face of mounting protests and revolutions throughout the Middle East, as a sign of U.S. weakness. Confidence in the United States as a stabilizing force is eroding, particularly in Egypt, while more traditionally hostile entities, like Iran and the Palestinian Authority, are becoming increasingly emboldened. This dramatic turn of events casts the U.S. role of peacemaker in grave doubt. That is but one reason why Israel must take firm hold of its own destiny, with a ready willingness to act decisively on its own behalf.

Israel: The Will to Prevail is a concise but detailed response to these events, including an analysis of the position Israel finds itself in today and an argument for the United States to reassert support for the State of Israel; an illustration of how history shows us Israel is often better off when she acts on her own behalf; and a road map for Jewish victory—achieved with or without backing from her allies. It's my hope that *Israel: The Will to Prevail* becomes a necessary part of the debate concerning the courses both Israel and her allies are likely to take. The book can serve as an outline for where the future leaders of Israel must stand in order to assure a permanent and secure Israel. The arguments presented will provide vital and practical information for every supporter of Israel.

The book is also the first to define the present moment and describe what Israelis of my generation and the next must do to preserve the nation they love. Israel has no choice but to act assertively when necessary, even if that means doing so on its own. A strong sense of Israeli nationalism must prevail if the state is to successfully overcome the current chaotic situation—even if that means contravening the wishes of U.S. administrations. Israel needs a new vision and direction; we need to take control of our own destiny and dictate our own history.

My own history is shaded by both conflict and a deeply rooted love for my country. My late father, Joseph Danon, fought in the Jordan Valley during a period of terrorists infiltrating Israel and was severely wounded in 1969 during the War of Attrition. His injuries contributed to his death a quarter of a century later. I was born two years later, 1971, the same year that the Palestine Liberation Organization (PLO) relocated to Lebanon and established a de facto state on its territory, which became a base for international terror organizations. I was a toddler in 1972, when the Munich massacre of Israeli Olympic athletes took place, and when the 1973 Yom Kippur War began. It would be several years before I understood what it meant when, in 1975, the United Nations passed a resolution defaming Zionism as racism. I consider myself a proud Zionist. I also know that people all over the world use that term as a pejorative—it doesn't matter that the Zionist resolution was repealed in 1991.

While the backdrop of my childhood in Ramat-Gan was one of ongoing external conflict, I had a loving home. My father had many difficulties from his injuries, including complete hearing loss and major physical issues. Despite these problems, he instilled in me the value of Israel by encouraging me to get to know the land and its people. Indeed, the story of my father is the story of the nation. He emigrated from an Arab nation to Israel via Italy because people could not come directly from an Arab state to Israel in the 1950s. His father ran a printing company, and his entire family fled the Arab states to go to Israel during the massive wave of immigration that occurred after 1948, leaving behind assets and property. The family had wanted to go before 1948, but it was impossible to do so before the establishment of the State of Israel because of the British Mandate, which restricted immigration.

There were two things that were fundamental in my house. The first was getting to know the land. Despite his severe disability, my father was successful in instilling me with the curiosity to learn about Israel's topography. I went on extensive hikes and camping trips from a very young age. While he could not join me physically, he interrogated me gently about what I saw and which roads I took. He knew every path and turn in the country from his service in the army—he was part of a reconnaissance unit. If I made a mistake, he would correct me—he would tell me better paths to take, shortcuts, and so on. After each trip, he would tell me the history of each location and what happened there a few hundred years ago and further back in biblical times. He was incredibly patriotic and his injuries only made him more, not less, devoted to Israel. He wanted me to appreciate the land as he did. By the time I was 12 or 13, I knew almost as much as he did about the land, and the stories connected with it.

The second fundamental was to develop the ability to take a stand. My father gave me the confidence to speak out at a young age. Because of his deafness and the fact that he never learned sign language, I often acted as translator during meetings at government offices because we had a special relationship—he developed the ability to read the lips and emotions of someone speaking in front of him, especially me. I was born after my father had sustained his injuries, but I learned how to communicate with him. On the way to these visits, he also told me to speak out, not to be quiet. According to him, if I had something to say, I should say it. Because of what his generation went through with wars, there was a great sense of optimism for my generation to achieve peace. Because of their own sacrifice, I think they had a naïve idea that a secure future for Israel had largely been achieved. But of course, we now know that this struggle is far from over.

In terms of dealing with Arab nations, many Israelis today have gone back to the warrior mentality of Ben-Gurion. We're sick of hollow accords and grand ceremonies done for the camera's sake. More of us are awakening every day to the fact that it takes more than a lovely ritual at the White House, with the accompanying smiles and handshakes and photo ops, to get anything real accomplished. Ben-Gurion was willing to pay a price for the security of Israel in international opprobrium, and so it is with a new generation of Israeli leaders. We also understand the necessity of shaping our fate by our own hands. If we have to pay a price with the United Nations, the European Union, and the United States, so be it.

Most importantly, Israel is a true strategic ally to the United States. It is a known axiom that Israel is America's cheapest and most effective aircraft carrier in the region. Aside from a small number of U.S. soldiers who were stationed in Israel to operate the Patriot air-defense system during the first Gulf War in 1990–1991, American soldiers have never had to deploy to defend the Jewish State. Israel has never made demands for concessions from the United States in return for strategic assets and access, as so many of Israel's allies have done. On the contrary, Israel regularly supplies the United States with anti-terrorism training and know-how and much-needed intelligence to keep the American people safe. Examples of this type of cooperation are too numerous to list, and mainly remain classified and unknown to most. However, one can only imagine the threats that would be posed today to America and U.S. interests, from both terrorist elements and belligerent states like Iran, if not for the high level of cooperation between these two allies.

I want to make a few important distinctions that you will find as you read the book. First of all, I do not use the common expressions often found in the media such as "occupied territories" and "West Bank." I prefer, as most Israelis do, to refer to this area as "Judea" and "Samaria" rather than as occupied territories. Instead of "settlements" and "settlers" I use the terms "Jewish communities" and "residents of these communities." "West Bank" is in fact a name that was created by Jordan after the War of Independence in 1948 when Arab armies overran Judea and Samaria. Despite the fact that Israel drove the occupiers back across the river during the 1967 Six-Day War, the term "West Bank" has entered the common lexicon. I reject it.

Also as you read you will encounter some familiar events—World War II, the creation of the State of Israel—and some lesser-known subjects—archeological Israel, the 1920 San Remo Conference. My intention is not to rewrite the entire history of

Israel; the point of *Israel: The Will to Prevail* is to make a case for an autonomous Israel, a secure Israel that should enjoy certain inalienable rights—the right to exist, the right to security, and the right to defend herself.

Finally, and perhaps most importantly, my book is a call to action to adopt a new, third way in dealing with the conflict we have suffered through for so many decades: a three-state solution to the Palestinian issue that engages both Egypt and Jordan, instead of the failed but familiar two-state proposal. The historical points I make are part of an effort to enlighten and to look at Israel in, for some of you, a new way.

I've devoted my life to working on Israel's behalf, including stints in the United States, where I worked with Diaspora Jews and fought propaganda and anti-Semitic activities on American college campuses. Today, as deputy speaker of the Knesset, chairman of the Immigration, Absorption and Diaspora Affairs Committee in the Knesset, as well as chairman of the World Likud Organization, I continue to work for a secure and peaceful Israel. *Israel: The Will to Prevail* is part of that effort. I want to engage people, especially those who disagree with me or who do not know enough about the region or who are misinformed about it. I'm not afraid to say what I think, even though there are many, including some in the Jewish community, who don't appreciate me rocking the boat. It would have been very easy for me to spend my time in the States talking about how nice the coastline of Israel is and how great the oranges taste. What good would that do? For example, I was against the Oslo accords since I believed it would be dangerous for Israel and I said so. This view wasn't greeted with open arms among my colleagues. But it turns out in retrospect I was right. You can't be afraid.

I'm also an optimist and I have great clarity of vision in terms of Israel and the Middle East. Therefore, I'm fine with attacks on my positions, even vicious ones. I've been the target of them, many times, from my opponents in the political arena and by some in the Israeli press, which, like much of the American press, leans left. I encourage those who disagree with my positions to debate their ideas with me. I am always willing to discuss the future of the land I love.

At many events I often get asked the question, why isn't Israel doing a better job on public diplomacy and public relations? I want to thank these people, the millions of supporters around the world who believe in and pray for us. All of the genuine lovers of Israel feel that they need tools to stand with us and to fight back against naysayers. I hope this book will help those who want to deliver the message about the Zionist miracle of the Jewish people in the land of Israel. I hope that *Israel: The Will to Prevail* helps all of those who wish to know and want to share my vision for Israel. In order to win any fight, you first have to position yourself on the stage. You cannot win a debate from your couch; you must speak out and use your knowledge and skills. I hope that this book will give you the urge to stand up and join the struggle for Israel with more knowledge and a better understanding of the reality in Israel.

. What follows is a beginning.

PART 1

DANGER AND OPPORTUNITY

THE CURRENT LANDSCAPE

DECADES BEFORE THE UNITED NATIONS CONFERRED SOV-ereign statehood on Israel in 1948, Jews in Israel and elsewhere had faced war, terror, and potential extinction. Today, a confluence of events has created a unique and perilous moment for Israel, and again she confronts possible vital threats from three interconnected sources: (1) instability in the region, including a nuclear Iran; (2) the U.S. administration's appeasement strategy in relation to Palestinian demands; and (3) an ideological war against Israel that has gained traction within the mainstream in recent years. In this first section, I examine these threats and outline how each, both inadvertently and by design, works together to undermine not only the security but also the very existence of

Israel. There is no other country in the world that has the legitimacy of its very existence questioned.

Israel's demise would be catastrophic for America and indeed for the world. It would mean losing a modern democracy in a region not known for social liberalism; and one that contributes so much to the world in terms of technology, science, art, and commerce. Let's not fool ourselves: The diminution of Israel would solve no problems in the Middle East, but would only embolden terrorists worldwide and increase the danger to other nations.

Israel's experience with Gaza demonstrates the folly of those who say that the only pathway to peace involves handing over our land to the Palestinians. When Gaza was given to the Palestinian Authority, Hamas was quickly voted in, in 2006. Since then no new elections have been held. Citizens who objected were shot in the street as a "message" to accept the regime or else. Gaza has also seen a dramatic and continued influx of smuggled weaponry from Egypt since Israel withdrew Jewish residents and soldiers in 2005. More than 12,000 rockets and mortars have been fired at Israel's Gaza belt communities from the enclave, and Israel currently sees increased rocket fire from Gaza every day. There are more tunnels running from Gaza to Israel, and the range of the rockets is much broader now than in previous years.

Despite this regular terror, the people in Gaza enjoyed great economic times in 2010 and 2011. The Palestinian Central Bureau of Statistics (CBS) put the rate of economic growth in Hamas-run Gaza at 31 percent for the second quarter of 2011, compared to same period in 2010, while unemployment fell to its lowest level for nearly a decade, to 25 percent. This sharp growth comes directly from the Israeli government's decision in June 2010 to maintain security status quo concerning Gaza while also loosening economic policies that allow for increased exports coming from terror-run Gaza. I believe this is appeasement at the expense of our own citizens' security and safety.[1] Terrorists may have achieved a level of confidence through economic security that enables them to ramp up their activities. This is the exact opposite of what was assumed would happen—fewer rockets.

Does Palestine have a right to exist as a separate entity? "Palestinians must abandon violence.... At the same time, Israelis must acknowledge that just as Israel's right to exist cannot be denied, neither can Palestine's," said President Obama in his June 4, 2009, Cairo speech. However, being a member of a group does not ipso facto mean that you should have a state. For instance, the Kurds live in Iraq, Turkey, Iran, and Syria. Stateless people in Europe (Romas), Estonia/Latvia (ethnic Russians), Thailand (Yao, Hmong, and Karen), and other places around the world often face tensions, but these issues will not be settled by granting statehood within the lands where they reside. In fact, it is rarely, if ever, suggested in these cases.

Furthermore, and this is basic, Israel cannot even begin to negotiate with a terror organization—it would be similar to the United States engaging with Al Qaeda. Nor can we engage with someone who does not recognize Israel as a Jewish state. How can you negotiate with someone who does not accept the 1948 borders of Israel, let alone the 1967 lines? We have to say very clearly that the first and most important pre-condition for any negotiation is accepting that Israel has a right to exist. If someone does not recognize you, they are actually getting ready for the next step, which, in this case, is military or terror attacks. The Obama administration can and has paid lip service to the notion that Palestinians and others in the region have to recognize the right of Israel's existence, but until the Palestinians actually do so—and to date that has not happened—why would any negotiation with Israel be seen as valid in their eyes?

The amount of Palestinian and other Arab hatred toward Israel—and, by the way, toward the United States—is due not to actions either Israel or the United States has taken. Instead, it is because generations of Palestinians, Iranians, Iraqis, Syrians, and others across the Middle East have been brought up to hate the entire Western world. Many educational systems in this region are dedicated to this proposition. "First the Saturday People, then the Sunday People" is an Arab saying that can be found spray-painted on walls in many Muslim neighborhoods. The "Saturday People" are, of course, Jews. Sunday people are Christians, who now find themselves victims of open persecution in the aftermath of the Arab uprisings.

I like to tell the story of three people who get lost in a forest. They come upon a hungry lion. Two of the friends decide to throw the third to the lion in order to satiate the beast. The next day, however, the lion is hungry again and is roaring threats. One of the remaining friends pushes the other to the lion, and the beast is satiated for a while. The following day, since there is no one left to protect the remaining friend, the lion eats him, along with a few deer and a couple of rabbits. It would have been smarter for the three to fight together to eliminate the threat at the outset: You can never satisfy or appease the appetite of a lion—it will always want more.

If you need proof that appeasement doesn't work, look at the 2005 terror attacks in London, or the 2008 terror attack in Mumbai. Neither had anything to do with Israel. They represent a pattern of attacks motivated by an insatiable desire to impose Islamic extremism around the world, and a total lack of tolerance for any other point of view. Islamic terrorists have carried out more than 18,000 attacks globally since 9/11.[2] More than 2,000 "successful" operations took place in 2011 (170 in October 2011 alone, in 16 countries, resulting in hundreds of victims representing five different religions, among them Islam itself). I'm not just speaking of those widely reported in Iraq and Afghanistan, but also less-publicized events in the Philippines, Thailand, Indonesia, India, Israel, Kenya, Nigeria, Somalia, Egypt, and Algeria. The list goes on and on and on. As of this writing, 43 attacks have been thwarted in the United States since 9/11,[3] including 14 in New York City alone.

I thought of these strikes as I traveled to South Sudan in August 2011, becoming the first Israeli elected official to show support for the new nation. The trip was meant to forge positive cultural and economic ties between Israel and the embryonic country's leadership. All students of international relations know that Africa in general, and Sudan in particular, is fraught with tension, famine, and, all too often, bloody warfare. While many factors drive these desperate conditions, the primary obstacle to peace and economic development in Sudan has been the presence of dictatorial Islamic forces committed to suppressing minorities and stifling contacts with the West. Sudan has been the scene of repeated mass killings, launched by this regime, rendering the south a place where lawlessness, rape, murder, and narcotics and weapons trafficking became the norm.

The establishment of this nascent nation, South Sudan, was born out of a sincere desire by the resident Christians to create a stable country modeled upon democratic values and an economy based on honesty and free trade. While the citizenry remains challenged by poverty, the decision by the people of South Sudan to join the community of democratic nations is a source of tremendous hope for a brighter future.

While much of the Western world responded with relative indifference to the creation of "yet another state" in Africa, I strongly feel that the creation of this new nation deserves the attention and admiration of the entire international community. President Salva Kiir Mayardit has had to fight Muslim extremists on the country's northern borders because they vehemently oppose coexisting with a Christian nation. This is further evidence for me that it is not Jews living in the Middle East that are "the problem." Islamic extremism and terrorism is an international problem: We are all a target for its violence.

Despite the fact that Israelis live in a tough neighborhood, and despite our enormous outlays for defense, we have managed to build a strong and vibrant economy without oil reserves; this is cause for consternation among Arab nations. They look at us, our modern and liberal society, and they don't like what they see. Moreover, what they see represents all of Western civilization. Israel just happens to be a handy target and a convenient scapegoat located on the front lines of Western society. It is a peril for all of us if we allow this grave situation to continue.

JIHAD AND THE GLOBAL THREAT

Israel has always been at the center of a storm. Case in point, I don't think enough people truly understand the difference in size of the Jewish State in terms of the totality of the surrounding Arab states. The total area of the State of Israel is 7,951.6 square miles and is bound by Egypt, Lebanon, Syria, Jordan, and the Mediterranean Sea. Egypt alone covers 386,659 square miles. Israel has a population of about 7.5 million people, and the Arab nations who surround her contain 369 million people. Once you have that in perspective, you may be able to understand that any "boiling over" from the Arab Spring, Islamic Jihad terrorists, and a nuclear Iran will have a direct and dangerous impact on Israel. Let me be clear up front: None of these threats will be eliminated or even mitigated by a two-state solution for Palestinians. This point will be thoroughly discussed in the last section of this book, but suffice to say that the commonly proposed "road map for peace" is unlikely to yield positive results for Israel and the democratic brotherhood of nations, and may, in fact, exacerbate an already dire situation.

I can say with certainty that as far as Islamic terrorists, Iran, Hamas, the Palestinian Authority, and the vast majority of Palestinians, including young but thoroughly indoctrinated schoolchildren, are concerned, there is only a one-state, one-ideology solution. Take a look at any map drawn by a Palestinian child, and also those found in textbooks, and you don't see Israel, only Palestine—in other words, Israel has been wiped from the map. Add unclear futures in Jordan, Syria, and Egypt, and the resultant synergy is cause for deep concern. To this combustible mix we must also figure in the threat Jihadi extremists pose to Israelis, Christians, and moderate Muslims alike.

A nuclear Iran greatly ups the ante, and poses an international dilemma all democracies have to face, Israel in particular. Many in the West have their heads in the sand about what nuclear power in the hands of a despotic regime means. One needn't look far back into history to see the horrific results of dictators who promoted hatred and incitement while trying to achieve military capabilities for mass destruction. Israel will not allow a second Holocaust to occur, and if required, I guarantee it will act unilaterally to remove an imminent threat. Indeed, Israel could lead the way in terms of providing strategic diplomatic and military solutions to counteract radical Islamic influence and aggression in our time.

To think that Iran is only a problem for the United States and Israel is, again, ignoring a bigger problem—the November 2011 attack on the British Embassy in Tehran should convince you of this fact. Innocent students did not storm the embassy as was suggested by some early reports; terrorists did.

To truly understand the threat that Israel and the West face, one must recognize the enemy. The enemy of Western democracy and freedom in the world today is undoubtedly Islamic fundamentalism, and the tool is Jihad. Jihad, meaning "to strive" or "to struggle" in Arabic, is a duty for Muslims. Jihad means fighting a war in the name of Islam, and the primary aim is the expansion and defense of the Islamic state. "Jihad" is derived from the root word "Jahada" (struggle). Jihad has come to mean an offensive war to be waged by Muslims against all non-Muslims to convert them to Islam. The Quran enjoins Jihad on all Muslims. Middle East historian Bernard Lewis points out that some modern Muslim sources try to portray Jihad in a spiritual and moral sense when addressing non-Muslims; however, historically it has only meant one thing.[4]

In Muslim tradition, the world is divided into two houses: the House of Islamic Peace (Dar-al-Salam), in which Muslim governments rule and Muslim law prevails, and the House of War (Dar-al-Harb), the rest of the world, still inhabited and, more importantly, ruled by infidels. The assumption is that natural law pits these two domains against each other, and the duty of Jihad is to continue the fighting until the world either adopts the Muslim faith or submits to Muslim rule. According to Lewis, "those who fight in the jihad qualify for rewards in both worlds—booty in this one, paradise in the next."[5]

The International Institute for Counter-Terrorism says that "offensive jihad" is an even more extreme interpretation of Jihad by former Egyptian Muslim Brotherhood ideologue Sayyid Qutb.

It is a radical belief that can "be employed for an offensive assault in order to reform societies by spreading Islam, and to liberate all men, both Muslim and non-Muslim."[6] The call for Jihad is defined as the following by Sheikh Abdullah Azzam (Shaheed), an influential Palestinian Sunni Islamic scholar and theologian, who was also a teacher and mentor of Osama bin Laden: "Where the Kuffar [infidels] are not gathering to fight the Muslims, the fighting becomes Fard Kifaya [religious obligation on Muslim society]," with the minimum requirement of appointing believers to guard borders, and the sending of an army at least once a year to terrorize the enemies of Allah. It is a duty of the Imam to assemble and send out an army unit into the land of war once or twice every year. Moreover, it is the responsibility of the Muslim population to assist him, and if he does not send an army he is in sin. And the Ulama, Muslim legal scholars, have mentioned that this type of Jihad is for maintaining the payment of jizya, a tax levied on an Islamic state's non-Muslim citizens. The scholars of the principles of religion have also said: "Jihad is Daw'ah with a force, and is obligatory to perform with all available capabilities, until there remains only Muslims or people who submit to Islam."[7]

The concept of Jihad is as old as Islam itself. According to American historian and writer Daniel Pipes, the Muslim prophet Mohammed engaged in an average of nine military campaigns a year, or one every five to six weeks; thus did Jihad help define Islam from its very dawn.[8] Conquering and humiliating non-Muslims was a main feature of the prophet's Jihad, and his successors continued conquering and subjugating non-Muslims. This empire spread across the Middle East, East and North Africa, and parts of southern Europe, including Spain. According to Islamic belief, these areas, once wrested from non-Muslims, could never become infidel territory again.

As I mentioned earlier, the greatest proponent of modern-day offensive Jihad was Sayyid Qutb, the leading intellectual of the Egyptian Muslim Brotherhood in the 1950s and 1960s. Qutb held extreme views about Jews and the West. In his book *In the Shade of the Qur'an* Qutb writes, "The Muslim world has often faced problems as a result of Jewish conspiracies ever since the early days of Islam."[9] Dale C. Eikmeier, a strategic planner at the U.S. Army War College, offers a broader definition of Qutbism, the theory espoused by Qutb: "a fusion of puritanical and intolerant Islamic orientations" that includes not only Qutb's ideas but also those of Abul Ala Maududi, Hassan al Banna, and even Shia elements, "to justify armed jihad in the advance of Islam, and other violent methods utilized by twentieth century militants. . . . Qutbism advocates violence and justifies terrorism against non-Muslims and apostates in an effort to bring about the reign of God. Others, i.e., Ayman Al-Zawahiri, Abdullah Azzam, and Osama bin Laden built terrorist organizations based on the principles of Qutbism and turned the ideology of Islamic-Fascism into a global action plan."[10]

One of Muhammad Qutb's students and later an ardent follower was Ayman Zawahiri, who went on to become a member of the Egyptian Muslim Brotherhood and later a mentor of Osama bin Laden and a leading member of Al Qaeda. Bin Laden himself was a great reader of Qutb and devoted his life to his teachings. According to Dr. Azzam Tamimi, director of the Institute of Islamic Political Thought in London, Qutb's writings "acquired wide acceptance throughout the Arab world, especially after his execution and more so following the defeat of the Arabs in the 1967 war with Israel."[11]

The greatest modern Jihad proponent in the Shiite world was undoubtedly Ruhollah Khomeini (1900–1989), a Shiite Marja and leader of the 1979 Islamic Revolution in Iran. Khomeini believed in a maximalist world-dominating Jihad, once saying that "establishing the Islamic state world-wide belong[s] to the great goals of the revolution."[12]

In a move that became common with Islamic fundamentalists, Khomeini had no problem supporting secular or non-Muslim terrorists and despots. Khomeini emphasized international revolutionary solidarity, expressing support for the PLO, the Irish Republican Army (IRA), and Cuba. Terms like "democracy" and "liberalism," considered positive in the West, became words of criticism, while "revolution" and "revolutionary" were terms of praise. In a speech Khomeini gave at Feyziyeh Theological School on August 24, 1979, he spelled out in simple terms what was incumbent on a Muslim: "Islam is a religion of blood for the infidels. . . . The great prophet of Islam in one hand carried the Koran and in the other a sword; the sword for crushing the traitors and the Koran for guidance."[13]

Soon after the Islamic Revolution began, on November 4, 1979, some Iranian students took over the U.S. diplomatic mission in Tehran. The students were supported by Iran's post-revolutionary regime, which was in the midst of solidifying power. They held 63 U.S. diplomats and three other U.S. citizens hostage (for a total of 66) until January 20, 1981. Of those captured, 52 were held until the conclusion of the crisis 444 days later. These actions violated the long-standing principle of international law that diplomats are immune from arrest and that diplomatic compounds such as embassies are considered the absolute sovereign territory of the occupying country as granted by the host country. As such, hostile incursions into the compound by elements of the host country are akin to acts of war.

Recently, the current Iranian president Mahmoud Ahmadinejad has repeated Khomeini's infamous words about destroying

Israel. Although many Western analysts who sympathize with Iran have translated the ayatollah's words as, "this regime occupying Jerusalem must vanish from the page of time,"[14] it is clear that the Iranian leadership has never intended for so passive a vanishing.

In Tehran, all official translations of Mr. Ahmadinejad's statement, including a description of it on his website, refer to "wiping" Israel away. Sohrab Mahdavi, one of Iran's most prominent translators, and Siamak Namazi, managing director of a Tehran consulting firm, who is bilingual, both say "wipe off" or "wipe away" is a more accurate translation than "vanish" because the Persian verb is active and transitive.[15]

When you couple these bellicose statements with Iranian leaders' call for "Death to Israel, America, and the UK," a slogan attached to missiles on display during military parades, few are unsure of the true nature of Iranian Jihadist intentions. The most interesting quotes attributed to Khomeini are the terms "Great Satan" and "Little Satan." While many in the West are still convinced that Jihad is being waged on them because of their support of Israel, the Jihadists claim the opposite is true. The terms were originally used by Iranian leader Ruhollah Khomeini in his November 5, 1979, speech when he accused the United States of imperialism and sponsoring corruption throughout the world. Israel was referred to as the "Little Satan," thus demonstrating whom the Jihadists really thought was in control. This is a total reversal of the wishful and ignorant thinking of those who say the United States is despised because of its ally Israel.

The greatest threats to the world are now found in the two streams of Islam, the Shiite and the Sunni. The Sunni form of Jihad as expounded by the likes of Al Qaeda, Hamas, and the Egyptian Gama'a al Islamiya has now provided for murderous attacks all over the world. The Shiite Jihadi trend, exemplified by

Khomeini, now has a successor in the form of Ahmadinejad, the present "mullocracy" in Iran, and its satellite terrorist groups like Hezbollah and Islamic Jihad.

The West has taken too long to understand the threat raised by Jihadists. David Selbourne, author of *The Losing Battle with Islam*, thinks that the West is well behind in its war against the Islamic fundamentalists for several reasons: the breadth and strength of the Islamic community is misunderstood, the influence of Islamic academic apologists, the use of the media, and the confusion of "progressives" about the Islamic advance.[16] We have to be willing to discuss the rise of Islamic rule in the Middle East and the rise of Islam in the West openly and honestly, without using politically correct euphemisms or hiding behind "polite" misinformation.

The fear and outrage that 9/11 precipitated seem like distant memories now. Even real threats such as the Underwear Bomber and the Times Square Bomber have become fodder for jokes on late night TV, and complacency has set in. But one thing we know for sure: There will be more of these attacks, and, eventually, "successful" ones.

Too often local authorities and the media downplay the link between global Jihad and so-called local incidents. For example, Mayor Michael Bloomberg of New York referred to Jose Pimentel, a Dominican-born Muslim convert also known as Muhammad Yusuf, as a homegrown "lone wolf" after he was charged with providing support for an act of terrorism as well as conspiracy and weapons charges. Pimentel was radicalized online, in part by reading *Inspire*, a Jihadi "lifestyle" magazine meant to encourage Jihad among its readers. Officials said that in October 2010 Pimentel also began to maintain a website dedicated to promoting radical Islamic ideology and support for violence against the

United States and that included links to Al Qaeda propaganda and instructional manuals.

Call this person a lone wolf if you want—but remember that today's radical Islam does not need tanks, armies, or even highly organized groups to radicalize soldier-followers who can and will do damage. I would prefer to call Pimentel and his ilk independent contractors in the war against the Western world. He may have physically acted alone, but he is part of a growing but dispersed ideologically driven army of soldiers who acquire arms easily and build bombs in basements and workshops. It's only a matter of time before such a terrorist succeeds, despite the excellent work of law enforcement, as has happened all over Israel, the Middle East, Africa, Asia, and Europe. Think of the young man in Toulouse, France, who shocked the sleepy city by allegedly assassinating a rabbi, his two young sons, and a girl outside of a Jewish school there. Just 23, Mohamed Merah is also suspected of killing three Muslim soldiers in southwestern France. Merah had become radicalized in a Salafist ideological group and seems to have solidified during two journeys he made to Afghanistan and Pakistan, according France's interior minister.[17] Reports indicate he acted alone, but again, his actions are part of a broad call by Jihadists to commit acts of violence. When you see something evil, you should not trivialize it; you should deal with it before it reaches your shores with more organized power.

At the end of the day, a simple quote from the Al Qaeda video claiming responsibility for the 2004 Madrid bombings that murdered 191 people and wounded 2,050 is the most telling about the Jihadists and their power. "You love life and we love death, which gives an example of what the Prophet Muhammad said," the video simply states.[18]

THE ARAB WINTER

The Arab Spring sounds romantic and poetic. After all, spring is associated with rebirth amid a world in harmony. And revolution sounds exciting and hopeful, especially in countries where the people are finally fed up with dictatorial leaders. But the Western view of these events is clouded by optimism and our own modern, liberal, give-them-the-benefit-of-the-doubt view of the world. From where I sit, I don't see it. First of all, revolutions often turn out very differently than their origins would have you hope or believe. It is not surprising that the Arab Spring of 2011 did not result in any roots of real democracy, nor any liberal revamping of what are extremely radical and narrow educational systems. As much as we long for peaceful reform throughout the region, we are likely to see more protracted turmoil, or worse. The major news organizations tend to encourage the desire we all have to see a positive outcome for the ongoing struggles in the region. But many incidents that are typically under-reported reveal a darker side to the ongoing conflict. For instance, Israel Radio reported in late November 2011 that King Abdullah of Jordan said "Israel has an expiration date" during an interview with the BBC.[19] Abdullah's comments were not widely reported outside of Israel and didn't create much of a stir in Europe and the United Kingdom, where anti-Semitism remains steady.[20] Let's take a hard look, country by country, at the current situation with regard to Israel's neighbors.

TUNISIA

The Muslim Brotherhood–linked Ennahda party enjoyed a landslide victory in the Tunisian elections in October 2011. Party leader and former exile Rachid Ghannouchi has expressed a

Jihadist vision for Tunisia and, I can only assume, the world as well. Ennahda's general secretary, Hamadi Jebali, is trotted out as the party's moderate and he may well be the next Tunisian prime minister. Yet on November 13, 2011, Jebali spoke at a rally in Sidi Dhaher, along with Houda Naim, a parliamentary deputy from the Palestinian party Hamas. Jebali referred to the period as "a divine moment in a new state, and in hopefully a 6th Caliphate," and that "the liberation of Tunisia will, God willing, bring about the liberation of Jerusalem."[21] While Jebali backtracked on the remarks later, I am skeptical—is this simply a taste of things to come from Tunisia and elsewhere in the Arab world? While it is officially illegal for Tunisians to speak to Israelis, which does not bode well for engagement with the country, the *Economist* reported that Ghannouchi recently met with Israelis in Washington.[22] Ghannouchi said that the constitution "would not bar further contact" with Israelis. Time will tell—we can only hope this is a sign of pragmatism and not simply happy talk. The Tunisian leader is considered by many to be "progressive" and "liberal" in terms of his interpretation of Islam,[23] perhaps a sign that we can resurrect the strong relationship that Israel had with the Tunisians in the past. Israel's hope is to go back to those days. At this point it's still too early to call since the messages from the Ennahda party are mixed, to say the least.

EGYPT

Israel's delicate peace treaty with Egypt, signed on March 26, 1979, is in peril as the Muslim Brotherhood has gained political ground in the country. In December 2011, the first round of elections in Egypt, 62 percent of eligible Egyptians voted. The Muslim Brotherhood came in first place with 36.6 percent, followed by the Salafist bloc with 24.4 percent. The Salafists are a militant group of extremist Sunnis who believe they are the only correct interpreters of the Quran. They also consider moderate Muslims to be infidels and seek to convert all Muslims to their fundamentalist version of Islam. Just because they call themselves peaceful right now doesn't mean that they won't turn Jihadist at some future time.

Egypt's final round of parliamentary elections since the overthrow of Hosni Mubarak gave an overwhelming victory to Islamist parties. The Muslim Brotherhood, which was banned but still active under Mubarak's regime, won the biggest share of parliamentary seats (38 percent). The Brotherhood's Freedom and Justice Party (FJP) has named Saad al-Katatni, a leading Brotherhood official who sat in the old parliament as an independent, as speaker of the assembly. The hard-line Islamist Al-Nour party came in second with 29 percent of the seats. The more liberal and secular New Wafd and Egyptian Bloc coalition came in third and fourth, respectively.[24] These results mean that Islamists will wield major influence over the country's new constitution, which will be drafted by the country's first freely elected parliament.

As for the prospect of establishing democratic values, we can only hope that the Brotherhood means what it says when it declares it wants good relations with the West and a revitalized and robust tourism business. However, one has to be concerned, judging not only from the history and ideology of the Muslim Brotherhood[25] but from the actions of the interim military rulers and recent events in Egypt.

Egypt has been slowly breaking relations with Israel to punish her for not yielding to Palestinian demands for a state. Shortly after Egyptian crowds stormed the Israeli Embassy in Cairo in September 2011, Egyptian prime minister Essam Sharaf and the Arab League secretary-general Nabil Elaraby, also an Egyptian, announced that the Camp David peace treaty isn't "sacred" and may have to be altered.[26] These views seem to reflect popular Egyptian opinion, according to a Pew Research Center poll published in April 2011. Fifty-four percent of Egyptians polled said their country should annul the treaty with Israel.[27]

On February 5, 2012, an explosion hit a gas pipeline running from Egypt to Israel, one of a series of attacks on the installation that crosses the Sinai region. The pipeline, which also supplies gas to Jordan, has come under attack at least 14 times as of this writing, since Egyptian president Hosni Mubarak was ousted. Gas pumping had to stop after the explosions, sometimes for many weeks.[28] Egypt's 20-year gas deal with Israel, signed during Mubarak's reign, is unpopular with some Egyptians because it is felt that Israel should pay more for the gas.

Egypt's Sinai Peninsula has become lawless, with both Bedouin and Islamist militants roaming far and wide. It is a tenuous situation and one Israelis do not deal with lightly; fighting with these militants could escalate into a much broader and more dangerous conflict. For example, in August 2011, militants dressed in Egyptian army uniforms killed eight Israelis on a highway leading to the city of Eilat in Israel; Israeli troops shot back. Defending ourselves resulted in the Israeli Embassy being stormed in Cairo. More altercations like this could irrevocably damage future Egyptian-Israeli relations.

The United States has cause for concern as well. In February 2012, Egypt's justice ministry accused 43 individuals, including 19 Americans, of illegally influencing Egyptian politics. Reports say the targets include the National Democratic Institute, the International Republican Institute, and other groups that promote human rights, a free press, freedom of religion, and political tolerance in countries around the world.[29]

There are many extreme examples of religious intolerance. Christians make up about 10 percent of Egypt's population of about 80 million people. They often complain that attacks against members of their community languish in the courts and police often turn a blind eye to discrimination or violence against them. Islamic fanatics have shot Christians in the streets with government troops standing idly by. On December 29, 2011, at least five people were hurt when a Muslim mob burned Christian homes in retaliation for a Facebook cartoon that hurt their feelings. On November 30, 2011, two Christian brothers were murdered by a Muslim group who rampaged through Christian homes and businesses. On October 9, 2011, military and Islamist gunmen massacred over two dozen Christians peacefully protesting a church burning in Cairo. On May 19, 2011, three Catholics were severely injured by a rock-throwing Muslim group who wanted to prevent a church from opening in Cairo; and on May 7, 2011, Muslim fundamentalists assaulted two churches with firebombs and gunfire, killing five Copts and seven others in an ensuing assault.[30] There are numerous other examples, as these are not unusual incidents. These are just episodes that are accounted for—many attacks go unreported.

Egypt's military leaders don't see that allowing a diversity of political voices to join the conversation is actually in its best interests. This is foolish since the military leadership is not popular within the country and taking a more open-minded approach could certainly help. U.S. secretary of state Hillary Rodham Clinton did warn Egypt's foreign minister that failure to resolve the dispute over the detained NGO workers, including 19 Americans, could lead to the loss of American aid—between $1.5 and $2 billion annually. This likely was an empty threat since aid gives the United States leverage with Egyptian leaders. The real question is will the new regime think it's worth forgoing aid—breaking ties with the United States and Israel, not to mention Western tourists—in pursuit of a pure Islamic state?

It's also disturbing and disheartening that the Obama administration has asked Sheikh Yusuf al-Qaradawi, the Muslim Brotherhood's leading jurist and a growing influence in Egypt, to mediate secret negotiations between the United States and the Taliban.[31] A report in the newspaper *The Hindu* states that President Obama wants the jurist to help him make a deal with the Taliban—enemies of the United States and Israel—as part of the sharia state the United States has been helping to build in Afghanistan. Both *The Hindu* and Reuters[32] suggest part of the negotiation would include the release of Taliban prisoners from Guantanamo Bay detention camp. Al-Qaradawi is the most influential Sunni Islamist in the world, mainly due to the wide dissemination of his ideas through mass media, including a television program on al-Jazeera TV called *Sharia and Life* and the website IslamOnline.net. He's not a gentle, Western-friendly fellow, so I'm not sure why the U.S. government would want to cozy up to him in this way. In fact, he is banned from the United States and Britain for supporting violence against Israel and American forces in Iraq.[33] For instance, in 2003, he issued a fatwa calling for the killing of American troops in Iraq:

> Those killed fighting the American forces are martyrs given their good intentions since they consider these invading troops an enemy within their territories but without their will. . . . Although they are seen by some as being wrong, those defending against attempts to control Islamic countries have the intention of *jihad* and bear a spirit of the defense of their homeland.[34]

Again, this is the kind of act that sends mixed signals to the Arab world and actually emboldens anti-Western Islamists. Any cooperation is an olive branch that will eventually be broken. The sheikh is also no friend of Israel, and his incitement has been a cause for concern for us for some time. According to former federal prosecutor and writer Andrew C. McCarthy, the sheikh likes to say what the West is loath to acknowledge: "the Jew-hatred that is endemic in Islam because it is rooted in scripture—not in modern grievances that could be satisfied if only the West changed its policies and Israel had the good grace to disappear."[35] In one al-Jazeera-broadcast sermon—not an isolated incident—al-Qaradawi prayed that Allah would kill all Jews: "Oh Allah, take this oppressive, Jewish, Zionist band of people. Oh Allah, do not spare a single one of them. Oh Allah, count their numbers and kill them, down to the very last one."[36] Why would you want to encourage someone who holds these views, particularly through official diplomatic means, and most especially as part of an effort to legitimize the Taliban? The Obama administration defends any effort to explore talks with the Taliban, even though it admits doing so presents risks. "The reality is, we never have the luxury of negotiating for peace with our friends," said Secretary of State Hillary Rodham Clinton about the initiative. "If you're sitting across the table discussing a peaceful resolution to a conflict, you're sitting across from people who you by definition don't agree with and who you may previously have been across a battlefield from."[37]

IRAQ

Despite all the sacrifices in blood and treasure expended by the United States and NATO, Iraq is not likely to emerge as a friend and ally to the West. No matter how many noble deeds have been enacted on their behalf, Iraqis take a dim view of outsiders who try to solve their internal and regional problems with force. Iran will also seek to keep its neighbor weak, constantly stirring up sectarian violence and promoting an ineffective government. Iraq may quickly degenerate into a semi-failed state and a launching pad for terrorists—or a fundamentalist Islamist state, which could be a more organized launching pad for terrorists.

Iraq's vaunted democratic institutions have always been fragile at best. Once again we see people bent on undermining them from the inside. Now that the United States has departed the country, a moral and ideological vacuum has emerged, and Islam can and doubtless will provide a new moral compass to the people. The United States Institute for Peace, an independent, nonpartisan conflict management center created by the U.S. Congress, predicts that "Sunni Islamism, long dormant and suppressed under Saddam Hussein, is highly likely to strongly re-emerge in Iraq, dominated by the Muslim Brotherhood, but rivaled in part by Wahhabi groups, partly stimulated by Saudi support, and partly reflecting the growth of more fundamentalist views elsewhere in the Muslim world."[38]

Fundamentalism has been steadily on the rise in the country. One chilling example was reported by Catherine Philp in *The Times* (London). A growing number of the 89 women in the Iraqi parliament are strident about sharia law. One of the women, Dr. Ubaedey, pledged that her first priority would be to implement sharia law. Philp explained that Dr. Ubaedey "found herself among an increasingly powerful group of religious women politicians who are seeking to repeal old laws giving women some of the same rights as men and replace them with Sharia, Islam's divine law."[39] The ominous title of the article? "Iraq's Women of Power Who Tolerate Wife-Beating and Promote Polygamy."

I don't hold out a lot of hope for relations between Iraq and Israel to improve. We have not had diplomatic relations since Iraq declared war on the newly established Jewish State in 1948 and to this day it does not recognize the State of Israel. Iraqi forces took part in actions against Israel in 1948, 1967, and 1973, and fired dozens of Scud missiles at Israel during the 1991 Persian Gulf War, despite the fact that Israel was not involved in that war. Israel bombed the Iraqi nuclear reactor at Osirak in 1981 under the belief that it was designed to create weapons, not energy. So our history has not been a good one and despite the fact that Iraqis have a democratically elected parliament, one of its first orders of business, in January 2012, was to vote on a bill that would ban Iraqis from traveling to Israel.[40]

TURKEY

Turkish prime minister Recep Tayyip Erdogan, once considered a friend to Israel, has had the audacity to demand that Israel apologize for the 2010 incident involving the Turkish Gaza-bound ship *Mavi Marmara*. In fact, the Turkish government owes Israel an apology for this attack, along with other recent actions that tried to de-legitimize Israel.

The "peaceful activists" aboard the *Mavi Marmara* sought to force their way through an Israeli blockade. They were, in fact, carrying a cache of illegal weapons, and they set upon the Israeli soldiers who had every right to inspect the flotilla. Israel said humanitarian aid confiscated from the flotilla would be transferred to Gaza, but that it would not transfer banned items found on board, such as cement. At first, aid was rejected by Palestinian authorities, but eventually they accepted the transfer, which was done under U.N. supervision.

There was a great deal of international condemnation and the United Nations called for an investigation. Israeli-Turkish relations also reached a low point after the event. The Turkish government seized upon this incident to boost its power and curry favor in the region. Erdogan promised to escort future convoys to Gaza with Turkish military vessels and to patrol the Mediterranean. He called the incident an "act of war," and promised to visit his "brothers" in Gaza. Our ambassador was expelled from Turkey, and the Turkish press took up the call to portray Israel as aggressive and barbaric.

Meanwhile, the "brothers" Mr. Erdogan refers to have the Hamas regime as their leadership, and have repeatedly called for the destruction of the Jewish State. The Hamas regime is so extreme that it condemned the assassination of Osama bin Laden, along with the leaderships of both the Muslim Brotherhood and the Taliban. Ismail Haniyeh, head of the Hamas administration in the Gaza Strip, told reporters that the group regards bin Laden's death "as a continuation of the American policy based on oppression and the shedding of Muslim and Arab blood." While noting doctrinal differences between bin Laden's Al Qaeda and Hamas, Haniyeh nonetheless added, "We condemn the assassination and the killing of an Arab holy warrior. We ask God to offer him mercy with the true believers and the martyrs."[41]

Relations between Israel and Turkey are now on a sharp decline, but it was not always so. In the early 2000s, the two countries enjoyed a mutually beneficial diplomatic partnership based on economic, military, and cultural agreements. Turkey was a popular vacation destination for Israelis, with more than a quarter million people traveling to the country annually. In fact, things were going so well that in 2008, Israeli prime minister Ehud Olmert asked Mr. Erdogan to mediate between Israel and Syria. The fact that Syria rejected the idea of mediation and conversation demonstrated just how quickly everything can change in a few years, and shows the instability of the region.

However, Turkey's current attitude toward Israel should not come as a surprise to those familiar with the Middle East. Since

Mr. Erdogan took office in 2003, his political agenda has become increasingly clear. His goal has been to flex his country's muscles and prove its ability to lead the Muslim world. Unfortunately, this has been done at Israel's expense.

The origins of Turkey's current problems with Israel can be traced back to 2004, when Turkey was rejected for membership in the European Union (EU). Mr. Erdogan warned of a rise in Islamic extremism as a result, stating that if Turkey was not welcomed into the EU, the country would pay a heavy price in continued and escalating violence from such terrorist groups as Al Qaeda and others. When European leaders did not take this threat seriously, the Turkish prime minister sought solace in the arms of the most radical anti-Western, anti-Zionist leader of all, Iranian president Mahmoud Ahmadinejad. Mr. Erdogan and Mr. Ahmadinejad have since grown close, as their regimes have found common ground when it comes to their foreign policies toward Israel. This relationship has proved to be a dangerous one for the entire region.

I would argue that Turkey, which once was a diplomatic ally, has become an epicenter of controversy and a foe to Israel. Turkey today competes with Iran in terms of who will lead the Arab nations. By choosing to ally itself with other dictatorial regimes throughout the Middle East, such as Hamas, Hezbollah, Sudan's genocidal dictator Omar al-Bashir, and the Islamic Republic of Iran, the Turkish government is clearly thumbing its nose at the United States and its core democratic and social values. This is a major problem because Turkey is a member of NATO and gets valuable information from the United States, which is problematic because they can use this information against Western and Israeli interests. This is a problem as we have seen in Egypt, which the United States has supported in terms of military equipment and technology. When nations become radicalized, you have to minimize your exposure to them. The Middle East is especially complex for Israel because the more radical you become against Israel, the most points you get in the Arab world—a dangerous form of "street credibility" that can help a radical nation rise in terms of power and danger.

SYRIA

Syria has long been the wild card of the Middle East and is likely to remain so. The expected collapse of President Bashar al-Assad's regime will leave a power vacuum that Iran will try to act decisively, if covertly, to fill. The Islamic Republic of Iran simply cannot afford to lose its closest and oldest ally—many analysts believe that a Sunni leadership in Syria would oppose Iran and Hezbollah. The furies Iran can unleash, together with its proxy army, Hezbollah, can wreak havoc on the region, and especially Israel and Lebanon. It's unclear what role Hamas would play in this situation. Hamas's leaders have described ties to the Syrian al-Assad government as a liability, and they have distanced themselves from Iran.[42] Syria reportedly received $1 billion from Iran in 2007–2008 to buy surface-to-surface missiles, rockets, anti-tank missiles, and anti-aircraft systems. In March 2008, an Israeli news service reported that Iran provided Syria with more than $1 billion for arms purchases, "reflecting Syria's drive to build up its military power . . . as well as the strengthening of ties between the two countries."[43]

Damascus is also a nest for most major terror organizations in the Middle East and the United States. With the collapse of the regime, Israel worries that the weaponry, including weapons of mass destruction, could be transferred to Hezbollah. At that point there will be no control over the area or the missiles. It will be easier for Hezbollah to use them, and of course they have more incentive to use them against Israel.

Again, the Obama administration early in its tenure sent mixed signals to the Syrians, causing both Egypt and Israel to worry. In 2009, the United States backtracked on sanctions, known as the Syria Accountability Act. The 2003 act, enacted by George W. Bush specifically because of Damascus's support for the militant groups Hezbollah and Hamas, targeted sales of spare aircraft parts, information-technology products, and telecommunications equipment. The Obama administration's moves toward rapprochement with the Assad leadership raised concerns in Israel and Egypt, as well as among some Syrian democracy activists. They worry that relieving pressure on Damascus would lessen its willingness to cut ties to Hezbollah and Hamas. "The regime feels very confident politically now," Ammar Abdulhamid, a Syrian democracy activist based in Washington, told a *Wall Street Journal* reporter at the time. "Damascus feels like it's getting a lot without giving up anything."[44] Things quickly went downhill in Syria from there, as witnessed by the Assad government's brutal attacks on its own people, particularly in 2011 and 2012. Demonstrating the zigzag in policy, in February 2012 the U.S. president, along with British prime minister David Cameron, called for "international unity against the regime's attacks on its own citizens," and possible extra sanctions against the region. The announcement was made as Syrian activists said Syrian government forces renewed bombardment of the rebellious city of Homs, where more than 400 people were killed in the first two months of February 2012 alone.[45]

IRAN

Iran is a country whose tentacles extend far beyond its borders. It is not just that Iran is going or has gone nuclear that is a problem— and I will come to that shortly. The loathing toward Israel and the West is a generational problem in Iran that will be very hard to fight even if the country is neutralized in terms of dangerous weaponry. The amount of hatred being delivered systematically to the young generation in schools every morning is breathtaking. We talk about national pride in Israel and the United States, and in Iran they do as well, with the added charm of ritual daily chants against the United States and Israel. In some schools students have to march over an American and Israeli flag before they enter their classrooms, and this includes Iranian Jewish children who attend public school. In Israel the children open the day with poetry and songs and in America they sing the national anthem.

Although Iran and Israel are enemies, Iran is also home to the largest number of Jews—estimates range from about 25,000 to 35,000—in the region after Israel.[46] Even Iranian Jews can get caught up in the unfortunate indoctrination of hate. They are forced, even though they may resist it privately, to publicly proclaim allegiance to the late Supreme Leader, Ayatollah Khomeini. Jews in Iran also have no access to postal service or telephone contact with Israel, and any Iranian who takes a chance and travels to Israel faces imprisonment and passport confiscation.[47]

It is obviously very difficult to know exactly what life is like for Jews in Iran, since they would naturally be hesitant to call attention to themselves or speak out against any persecution or discomfort, but the *Human Rights Activists News Agency* provides a clue. It reported that Adiva Mirza Soleyman Kalimia and her husband Varjan Petrosian were hanged on March 14, 2011, at Evin Prison.[48] The report noted that the executions were done secretly. Kalimia was born in Jerusalem in 1956 to an Iranian-Jewish family, said reports. She lived in Miami for several years and visited Iran three times before being arrested and put in prison, allegedly for adultery, a convenient accusation when Iranian authorities want to rid themselves of whomever they consider to be undesirable. According to the report, three other people, including one woman and two men, were also executed at the same time. I assume these facts don't represent what Roger Cohen meant when he wrote in a *New York Times* column in February 2009 that "the reality of Iranian civility toward Jews tells us more about Iran—its sophistication and culture—than all the inflammatory rhetoric."[49]

The treacherous alliance between Iran and Venezuela does not augur well for the United States. Hugo Chavez's hatred of the United States has nothing to do with Jews, but it still has an impact on Israel. According to the U.S. State Department's country report on terrorism that covers 2009, "President Chavez continued to strengthen Venezuela's relationship with state sponsor of terrorism Iran. Iran and Venezuela continued weekly Iran Airlines flights connecting Tehran and Damascus with Caracas."[50] Moreover, these are not commercial flights with registered passengers. It is safe to assume that not only materials and technology, but militants as well, are being transferred—all of which are surely used against the interests of Central and South America, and the United States.

In 2010 I was in Colombia. I met the former president Uribe Velez at his residence as part of a delegation of the Israeli Foreign Affairs Ministry. He presented a map and pointed out the border area between Venezuela and Colombia. I said, yes, it's the jungle. "No, it's not," he corrected. "They are camps for Hezbollah warriors being trained by Iranian military personnel." As we spoke, it became clear to me that the planes were delivering military personnel and equipment. Chavez wants to become a stronger force in South America by spreading anti-Western, anti-American ideology. So, on the one hand, this very important example seems to have nothing to do with Israel, but, on the other hand, you see the linkage—it is in fact a tightly constructed web. For example, there was a bomb attack on the Israeli Embassy in Buenos Aires on March 17, 1992, in which 29 civilians died and 242 were injured. On July 18, 1994, Buenos Aires's Jewish community center, Asociación Mutual Israelita Argentina (AMIA), was bombed and 85 people died, with hundreds of others injured. It was proven that the explosive materials were delivered by Iran to the Iranian Embassy and from there they were funneled to the terrorists.

Iran has also used the Arab Spring or uprising to become more vocal and aggressive. In November 2011, the Iranian Revolutionary Guards auxiliary, Basij militia, issued a statement where, for the first time, it outlined its end game. It said Iran's Supreme Leader, Ayatollah Ali Khamenei, had been divinely chosen to impose Islam on all parts of the world.[51] The goal of the regime is to destroy America and Israel as part of the Muslim "awakening" (or the Arab Spring) moving throughout Africa and the Middle East. The statement was made in response to the invasion of the Israeli Embassy in Cairo, which it called a "nest of spies." The Basij statement says both America and Israel will be destroyed and Islam's conquest of the world will begin.

Iran has stepped up its ambitions in recent months and will soon have the capability to build nuclear bombs. A report by the International Atomic Energy Agency (IAEA) released in November 2011 stated that Iran has been engaged in "activities relevant to the development of a nuclear explosive device."[52] This was the most strongly worded IAEA report on Iran to date. It also coincided with reports in the Israeli press that the Israeli government was considering a preemptive strike against Iran's nuclear facilities, as we have done successfully in the past in Iraq.

According to Nicholas Blanford, writing in the *Wall Street Journal*, Brigadier General Masoud Jazayeri, the deputy chief of the country's armed forces, was quoted saying that "the smallest action by Israel" will result in "its destruction," adding that plans for retaliation were already in place.[53] Blanford continues:

> Many analysts believe that those plans could include directing Hezbollah to unleash its military might against Israel, pummeling it with thousands of long-range rockets, placing the Jewish state's heartland on the frontline for the first time since 1948. . . . The rate of recruitment into Hezbollah's ranks has soared. New recruits are bused to secret training camps in the Bekaa Valley, where they endure lengthy marches over the craggy limestone mountains carrying backpacks weighed down with rocks. They learn fieldcraft and weapons handling, and some go on to receive advanced training in Iran. The military instruction is interspersed with religious and cultural lessons, teaching them the importance of jihad, martyrdom and obedience to Hezbollah's religious figurehead, currently embodied by Ayatollah Ali Khameini, the supreme leader of Iran.

When there is a leader committed to the conviction of hating the Jewish people who is also close to or has developed the technology to demolish a nation, we cannot be silent. Compare the period of Nazi Germany to what is happening in Iran and you will find many similarities, from a messianic leader to national unification via hatred and propaganda. The lack of firm action and the dialogue of the international community are very similar to those in Europe before the Second World War. There isn't time to wait and see what the Iran scenario will turn out to be. By then it will be too late.

Diplomacy and more international pressure doesn't seem to do much to distract Iran from its single-minded mission to build a nuclear weapon. Nor has the official policy of unconditional engagement with Iran that the Obama administration has fruit-lessly pursued.[54] There are ways to deal with the Iranian threat that take a strong will and the fervent desire to overcome the Iranian nuclear and military threat once and for all. The assassinations of Iranian nuclear scientists, reports of which make the news peri-odically,[55] are stop-gap measures carried out by a range of inter-national players. They do not deal with the main issue of stopping the nuclear program. There will always be more scientists.

The imposition of crippling sanctions that would be felt by the Iranian people in their daily life in a way that current sanctions are not felt would be the first course of effective action. There has been some headway in this direction recently. In January 2012, the European Union imposed a phased ban on oil purchases from Iran. The ban covers imports of crude oil, petroleum products, and petrochemical products. It also covers the export of major equipment and technology for the sector. The European market accounts for a fifth of Iran's oil exports; its biggest importer is Italy.[56] While these sanctions may prove harmful to Iran, it's also crucial to note that these sanctions do not stop the flow of Iranian oil into Asian markets. According to the U.S. Energy Information Administration, Iran's top export destinations in 2010 were China, with 20 percent of exports; Japan, with 17 percent; India, with 16 percent; and South Korea, with 9 percent.[57]

At the same time, the United States expanded sanctions to include the country's third-largest bank. "At a time when banks around the world are cutting off Iran and its currency is depre-ciating rapidly, today's action against Bank Tejarat strikes at one of Iran's few remaining access points to the international finan-cial system," the treasury undersecretary for terrorism, David S. Cohen, said in a statement. "Today's sanction against Bank Tejarat will deepen Iran's financial isolation, make its access to hard currency even more tenuous, and further impair Iran's ability to finance its illicit nuclear program."[58] On February 6, 2012, the United States finally put these stricter sanctions into effect. They give U.S. banks new powers to freeze assets linked to the Iranian government and close loopholes that officials say Iran has used to move money despite earlier restrictions imposed by the United States and Europe.[59] I commend the Obama administration's efforts on this front, but I also worry it's too little too late.

Let us hope that such sanctions make it difficult, and perhaps impossible, for companies to pay for oil purchases—about 45 percent of the government's budget came from oil and natural gas revenues[60]; crude oil accounts for 83 percent of the total value of its exports. This would put a major financial dent in Iran's nuclear weapons program. It would also severely impede Iran's ability to fund terror training and attacks in the region and around the globe.

With such sanctions comes increased tension and potential violence. This is when the will and stomach to continue with tight measures against the regime is tested. For instance, perhaps as a response to sanctions, Iran stepped up its terror attempts abroad. In February 2012, Israeli Embassy workers in the capital cities of both India and Georgia were targeted in terrorist attacks that officials in Israel believe were planned and carried out by Iran along with the militant group Hezbollah. The bomb in Tbilisi, Georgia, was defused before it could do any damage, but the suspected magnetic bomb in New Delhi, which was placed by a man on a motorbike onto an embassy worker's car, exploded and injured at least two, including a female Israeli diplomat.

It is not unreasonable to imagine this will happen on American soil at some point in the not-too-distant future. Indeed, in Senate testimony in January 2012, Director of National Intelligence James Clapper said Iranian officials "are now more willing to conduct an attack in the United States in response to real or perceived U.S. actions that threaten the regime." It would not be anything new—in 2004 the U.S. State Department deported two security guards attached to the U.N. Iranian mission after they were caught conducting surveillance of city subways and landmarks. Iran's U.N. mission allows officials from Iran's Ministry of Intelligence to live and move freely in New York under official diplomatic cover.[61]

There are other sanctions that would be felt by the people, making them more likely to continue to rise up against the oppressive regime and demand change in the region.[62] Treating Mr. Ahmadinejad like a celebrity at venues like Columbia University and the United Nations must cease. In fact, travel restrictions should be put in place for all Iranians. Right now there are cheap daily round-trip flights between the United States, Europe, Asia, and Tehran. Stopping many of those flights would indeed have a crippling effect on Iran. This may seem unrealistic to many, but frankly, it is the kind of restriction that would strike at the heart of Iranian society. It is also not that dissimilar to the sanctions against apartheid South Africa. For example, restrictions on travel to South Africa in the 1980s contributed very effectively to the isolation of the country. So why not do the same in terms of travel to and from Iran?

Despite the fact that many nations, like China and Russia, condemn Iran for its human rights record and for promoting hatred, they are eager to sign more economic agreements. China and Russia in particular have complained recently about further sanctions against Iran and, in fact, ignore many of those already in place. In fact, Russia has dismissed the most recent IAEA report as "biased and unprofessional."[63]

People, including many in the U.S. administration, are afraid these kinds of tough sanctions on Iran would cause the cost of oil to go up, but I believe the world could deal with any incremental rise in prices. Even though Iran is the fourth-largest producer of crude oil, according to Global Security, a military and technology information organization, and averages about 3.72 million barrels per day, it holds only 90 billion barrels of proven oil reserves, or just about 9 percent of the world total.[64] In short, the world could survive without Iranian oil.

If these sanctions don't work, and the Iranian government continues to move closer to weaponization, we need to completely neutralize the nuclear threat. This means neutralizing reactors well before they are active; for obvious reasons it is much harder to neutralize an active reactor. This should be a joint effort led by the United States and Western countries with Israel, because a joint effort sends a strong statement and underlines the fact that Iran presents a global threat. However, Israel could do it alone, if necessary. It's not clear whether Iran would be suicidal or not in terms of firing a nuclear weapon if it had its hands on one. Israel is not in a position to gamble on this issue.

THE OBAMA ADMINISTRATION AND
THE DIPLOMATIC TSUNAMI

It's an unfortunate fact that Israel has grown more distant from the United States, and I believe this puts both our countries in peril. The relations between the United States and Israel have been at times contentious, as I outline in detail in the next section, but the air has definitely grown chillier between the two governments since the Obama administration took office.

From the beginning of President Obama's tenure he made a series of missteps. The first was perhaps his willingness to accept the Nobel Peace Prize for the Middle East peace process a few weeks after his inauguration. This cart-before-the-horse move was a purely political act on the part of the Nobel committee and Obama should have seen it for what it was. A polite and grateful decline would have been more appropriate so that the world could wait for the results of his foreign policy.

The second error he made was in his address to the Muslim world in his Cairo speech of June 2009. In it he expressed a wishful-thinking vision of peace that was naïve and that dangerously lifted the hopes of Palestinians. Obama reiterated his support of a Palestinian state, and he firmly rejected any construction by Israel of new communities in Jerusalem, Judea, and Samaria, thereby going to the side of Palestinians and their demands.

People in the region viewed the speech as a sign of weakness. While the president was trying to build new bridges to the Arab world, his approach underscored the fact that this administration seems not to understand the Arab mind. As someone who lives in the Middle East, I know that respect is won in two ways: by showing strength and honoring yourself. The president did neither. After 9/11 President George W. Bush's approach was to confront radical Islam head-on. President Obama was trying to open a new era between the two civilizations that was less confrontational. He thought, by reaching out to the Arab world, he would be able to build a new path based on dialogue and understanding—and maybe to calm down the atmosphere. But it didn't work because the Muslim world is not something that can be affected or moved by words. In fact, I would argue the opposite happened, and the fundamental sectors of the Islamic world were in fact galvanized and bolstered. Of course, there are elements within the Arab community who are pro-Western and understand the benefits, but the other strong elements of radical Jihadists and other extremist forces are not moved by any speech or outreach that comes from Western society. It is dangerously naïve to think that a charismatic speech would be able to bridge or narrow the clash of civilizations.

The third and most crucial mistake Obama made was to adopt many of the demands of the Palestinians, unlike other presidents, who tried to play the role of the mediator between the two parties.

Perhaps this was because such mediation resulted in few results—I am thinking, for example, of 1991, just after the first Gulf War, when President George H. W. Bush called a conference in Madrid between Israel and the Arab nations that were directly involved in the conflict. Talks continued afterward in Washington, but nothing substantial was accomplished. Then, in 2000, President Bill Clinton convened a peace summit between Palestinian president Yasser Arafat and Israeli prime minister Ehud Barak. Barak was willing to compromise on all major issues, including going back to 1967 lines and compromising part of Jerusalem; however, Arafat was not willing to continue and in fact walked out of the talks. When Barak returned to Israel he was thanked by being booted out of office.

Perhaps the Obama administration decided it was more expeditious to simply adopt the demands of the Palestinians by calling, in May 2011, for a return to the 1967 borders and the division of Jerusalem (see Appendix E). In his May 2011 speech on the Middle East at the State Department he said, "We believe the borders of Israel and Palestine should be based on the 1967 lines with mutually agreed swaps, so that secure and recognized borders are established for both states." This statement made the Palestinians feel as if they no longer have to negotiate, and that they should win all their demands at no cost or concessions whatsoever. What President Obama did with that statement was to accept borders that are often described as "Auschwitz lines": indefensible borders that would put Israel in an untenable position, easy to attack from all directions. Moreover, a withdrawal to 1967 borders would mean a forced evacuation of over 300,000 Israelis. Is this realistic or even desirable?

This was done without insisting that the Palestinians recognize Israel or make a concerted effort to end incitement. In fact, President Obama didn't ask for any compromise on the Palestinian part. In other words, the Palestinians want recognition of their state without ever having to recognize the State of Israel. President Obama provided a tall and convenient ladder to climb toward this goal, and it is going to be very hard to bring them down. It was an effort to build confidence in the Arab world; it was his way of saying, we don't automatically side with the Israelis. Look what has happened in Egypt, Syria, Libya, Tunisia, Yemen, and the region since then. The Middle East has its own dynamic and doesn't run according to guidelines set in Washington.

Many people on the left claim that because technology allows missiles to be sent over great distances there is no meaning to holding land—the idea being that Israel can defend itself with advanced weaponry. This is a bizarre stance. First, because we have Jewish communities who live in Judea and Samaria, abandoning that area for the Palestinians would be morally irresponsible. Second, it is very important to have a presence on the ground for safety reasons. When we see today the proximity of Gaza to people living in Israeli communities the problem is clear. Our people are attacked on nearly a daily basis by short-range missiles. Going back to 1967 borders, also known as Armistice lines, would put millions of Israelis who live on the coastal areas at risk via homemade missiles and other weapons. We can and will deal with Iran and other aggressive countries, but why create a safe haven for terrorism in our backyard?

In the Jordan Valley we have always understood the need for developing civilian communities and a constant military presence, going all the way back to the 1967 lines. If you abandon your military hold in the Jordan Valley, you create a land linkage between the Palestinians and Jordan and others in the Arab world. Jordan allowed Iraqi soldiers to come through their land in 1948, for example. Creating a Palestinian state, especially one based on 1967 borders, would create a passage between Judea and Samaria and Jordan that Iranians would use to get into Israel and create havoc. With all due respect to international forces, we learned in Lebanon that international forces couldn't come close to our own military people in protecting an area from terror.

JERUSALEM

Israel's decision in September 2011 to approve construction of 1,100 homes in the Jerusalem neighborhood of Gilo was called "counterproductive" by the Obama administration. State Department spokeswoman Victoria Nuland said, "We consider this counterproductive to our efforts to resume direct negotiations between the parties and we have long urged both parties to avoid actions, which could undermine trust, including in Jerusalem, and will continue to work with parties to try to resume direct negotiations."[65] First of all, can you imagine saying no African Americans should build houses in the South, or in Harlem, or Chicago? By taking the position that Jews should not build in any part of "East Jerusalem," the American administration seemed to mix up the Palestinians' claims to "East Jerusalem" with their claims to Judea and Samaria. Because the Obama administration has not distinguished between building Jewish residences within Jerusalem versus communities in Judea and Samaria, it has basically sided once again with the Palestinians against Israel on a critical issue.

Jerusalem was liberated along with Judea and Samaria, but unlike Judea and Samaria it was unified or annexed immediately, and since then we do not see a difference between any part of Jerusalem and any part of Israel—in other words, Jerusalem is part of Israel. Previous administrations never officially approved this policy but de facto it was a done deal. Israelis built everywhere in Jerusalem. The Obama administration put pressure not to build in so-called East Jerusalem. This is another first, because previous administrations and presidents have taken the official approach of not publicly encouraging building in the eastern part of Jerusalem, but it was a fact of life that was accepted. You have huge Jewish neighborhoods in so-called East Jerusalem, including Gilo and Ramot, and in any scenario those neighborhoods would be part of Israel. Personally, I believe Israelis have the right to build and live in every part of Jerusalem. Even those on the left in Israel condemned President Obama's speech because Gilo is not a disputed area. Mr. Obama placed a major part of Jerusalem on the same level as Judea and Samaria and ignored the reality on the ground. Every Jew sees Jerusalem as the essence of Zionism; Jews pray in the direction of Jerusalem. Even those people on the left in Israel see it this way. I don't argue with the fact that there is contention over setting sovereign boundaries around Jerusalem and in Judea and Samaria. However, every single peace plan that's been proposed for decades leaves Gilo and other Jewish neighborhoods of eastern Jerusalem on the Israeli side.

Gilo also happens to be an important symbol of the Israeli resistance during the Second Intifada, when Arab snipers fired at

Gilo Jews from the village of Beit Jala. Jewish residents began to evacuate and then, finally and belatedly, the Israeli government provided cement barriers and bulletproof glass to protect Gilo residents. *Not* building in Gilo basically means allowing a Palestinian ring around Jerusalem.

Moreover, Jerusalem is not a settlement. It's the capital of Israel. Jews have been living in Jerusalem continuously for more than three millennia and now constitute the largest single group of inhabitants, and have since the nineteenth century. It is, in fact, important that Israelis control Jerusalem in terms of international relations. Many people from various places come to visit the holy sites, including Christians who come to pray. If Israel does not control the city, it may well be impossible for Jews to practice and pray there; likewise it would be very difficult for Christians to come and feel comfortable. This is being proven in Bethlehem, which is under the control of the Palestinian Authority. Yes, Christians are allowed to go but they do not like to sleep there, nor do they feel comfortable.

Another scenario that has been presented is to have an international group of supervisors, like the United Nations, oversee parts of Jerusalem. This is an incredibly foolhardy idea since such groups would be too easy to manipulate—and at any rate they would have no real authority to act on aggressive activities. Drive three hours from Jerusalem to the northern border and you'll see U.N. peacekeeping forces taking pictures of Hezbollah gearing up for the next conflict. It would be the same if the United Nations were controlling the holy sites of Jerusalem. The only thing they could do is to take pictures of potential threats—they could do nothing physically about them. The last thing we want to see is international inspectors telling Jews or Christians where it is safe and not safe to pray in the old city of Jerusalem. The only way there will be real freedom of religion in Jerusalem is if Israel is in charge, as is happening today.

I respect the freedom of religion of Muslims and Christians, and we have to do whatever we can to allow freedom of religion to flourish. Christians and Muslims enjoy many more rights in areas under Israeli protection than in areas under Palestinian or Jordanian control. According to the Oslo Accord, Palestinians agreed to ensure free access to a specific list of Jewish religious sites located in parts of Judea and Samaria. Jewish sites like the Tomb of Joseph, under Palestinian control, are supposed to be open for Jews to pray, but in fact, they are not, and the Tomb of Joseph is desecrated on a regular basis. When I go there, it has to be at night with a heavy army escort. It is simply too dangerous during the day. Palestinian policemen have shot people who have tried to get into the tomb without coordinating it first with an army escort. For instance, on April 24, 2011, Palestinian police shot and killed one Israeli and wounded four others after they quietly visited Joseph's tomb. Officials on both sides confirmed the incident. The reason for the murder was because the group of Israelis failed to coordinate the visit with Israeli military and Palestinian police officers. Freedom of religion should be a two-way street.

I remember my parents telling me that prior to 1967 if they and my grandparents, who were observant Orthodox Jews, wanted to look at the old city of Jerusalem, which contains many important Jewish, Christian, and Muslim religious sites, they had to go to the roof of a building on the western side of the capital, since the old city was in the Jordan-controlled eastern side. My parents, along with many other Jews, could not pray at the Wailing Wall, since there was no access at all. Today, that's different. I am a strong believer in connecting people from all over the world to Jerusalem by having them come and learn the history—because once you understand Jerusalem, you understand the internal connection of the Jews to the land of Israel. When you are in the Jewish Quarter or at the Western Wall, one really feels the holiness of the whole city.

A FREEZE ON RELATIONS

In November 2009, Prime Minister Netanyahu announced a ten-month freeze on building that excluded eastern Jerusalem. This was before Vice President Joseph Biden's March 2010 visit to Israel. In order to show goodwill to the United States, in November 2009, Prime Minister Netanyahu imposed a ten-month freeze on building in Jewish communities in Judea and Samaria, which meant that even if you bought the land and had a permit, the government said you could do nothing for ten months. That was a major mistake. The demand of the settlement freeze is a new issue of the Obama administration—previous administrations had not done it. Further, during the negotiations prior to Netanyahu's second term, the American and international demand for a settlement freeze was not accepted. Barak negotiated with Egyptian president Mubarak and Palestinian leader Yasser Arafat. President Clinton facilitated the natural growth of settlements. This growth was also accepted during George W. Bush's administration, and was in fact facilitated by that administration.

Netanyahu paid a political price for this since many in the Likud party were not happy with the freeze and criticized him harshly for it. He tried to show goodwill, but ultimately instead of getting a pat on the back from the American administration, he was rebuked by it. The freeze set a terrible precedent since first it was against the will of the voters who had brought the Likud party into a leadership position. And such a freeze is against the DNA of the Likud party. It was also a brutal interference of the government on rights of citizens who live in Judea and Samaria because it was enforced on government projects as well as on private owner land projects. It would be similar to the U.S. government enforcing a building freeze on people who owned land legally and paid taxes on it.

The U.S. State Department issued a statement thanking Netanyahu for placing a freeze on building, but when the regional committee automatically approved construction of new housing in Gilo, an area that is obviously part of Jerusalem, Netanyahu received a slap in the face. President Obama gave an interview to Fox News while visiting China in November 2009 in which he said such building was "dangerous" for Israel, adding, "I think that additional settlement building does not contribute to Israel's security. I think it makes it harder for them to make peace with their neighbors. I think it embitters the Palestinians in a way that could end up being very dangerous."[66] This quote shows that there is a serious lack of understanding on the part of President Obama or his advisors.

Meanwhile, during the freeze Palestinians did not go back to negotiations so it was a useless and unfortunate exercise that negatively impacted many Israelis. I do not accept the opinion of those in my party who said the freeze was goodwill. It was instead a mistake that ultimately labeled and hurt the communities in Judea and Samaria, and we did not get anything in return. Once you show the weakness of compromise, you cannot make demands for compromise from the other side. On the contrary. The other side generally sees a wide opening to push for more concessions.

I argued with the prime minister, with whom I work closely on other political and economic issues. This was not easy since Prime Minister Netanyahu is the leader of my party. I was trying to convince my party to oppose the freeze, but for some it was hard politically to speak out. The main reason I was against the freeze was not because there wouldn't be houses built but because we were labeling Jewish communities and accepting the terminology of "settlements" as an obstacle to peace.

We have a Likud faction meeting every Monday at 2 p.m. when we decide about the weekly affairs of the party. One meeting after the freeze decision, I told Prime Minister Netanyahu that the decision was contrary to the wishes of the people who voted for us. A few ministers privately said, outside of the public meeting, that they were proud of me. In fact, the majority of Likud members were against the freeze but they were not willing to step up and oppose it publicly. I walked into a political fight that led to many events and campaigns. For instance, I was one of the organizers of a mass rally to protest the freeze. I also gathered enough signatures to call a special meeting of the central committee of the party to vote against the settlement freeze. The motion to support Jewish communities and renew building passed unanimously in the central committee—sending a strong message to the ministers within the government. One of my reasonings against the freeze was that after ten months the U.S. administration would ask for another ten months, and that is exactly what happened.

In September 2010, world sponsors of the so-called Middle East peace process called on Israel to extend the building moratorium. According to a statement "the Quartet," which includes the United States, the European Union, the United Nations, and Russia, released, they asked Prime Minister Benyamin Netanyahu to extend the ten-month settlement freeze that would expire at the end of that month. "The Quartet noted that the commendable Israeli settlement moratorium instituted last November has had a positive impact and urged its continuation," the statement read. President Barack Obama and Hillary Clinton had previously urged Netanyahu to extend the freeze.[67] The Palestinians said they would drop out of the peace talks unless the freeze continued. I'm not sure that would have been possible because the fact is Palestinian Authority leaders ignored the freeze gesture for several months and were only willing to begin peace talks as the construction freeze drew to a close, demanding that it continue. When construction resumed after the freeze was over, the Palestinian Authority left talks and did not return.

To be clear, the freeze was not on new communities but on natural growth. Nevertheless, the prime minister came back to Israel, where he announced he was considering the extension of the freeze. In return for the extension, Israel would reportedly get sophisticated aircraft, loans, and a list of other trade-offs. It was never made clear whether the aircraft would be free. I gathered all my energy and the commitments I had gotten previously. I had lost the first fight but I did not want to lose this one. We decided to hold a major event at a construction site in the hills of Samaria, marking the end of the freeze. Later reports clarified that the United States was not willing to offer any of the commitments that had been suggested. Reports at the time cited one of our diplomats accusing U.S. secretary of state Hillary Clinton and U.S. president Obama of pulling a bait and switch on Netanyahu, with Clinton making these promises but then rescinding them after talks of a second freeze went public and the idea lost steam on both sides. While the second freeze talks continued, the prime minister was off the hook, with little pressure to return to the negotiating table. An Israeli journalist suggested that Palestinian Authority chairman Mahmoud Abbas had planned all along for the talks to break down and was hoping not for a negotiated settlement but for an international agreement on the borders of a Palestinian state.[68]

If that was indeed part of Abbas's plan, he saw some success as both Argentina and Brazil said they would recognize a Palestinian state on all the land east of the 1949 armistice line.[69] That territory is home to approximately 500,000 Jews, along with up to 1.5 million Arabs, and includes historically Jewish towns as well as the Temple Mount, the Tomb of the Patriarchs, and Rachel's Tomb, Judaism's first, second, and third most holy sites, respectively.

So I thought, okay—the period of the first freeze was finally over. My strategy was to gather members of the Likud, myself included, and go to one of the religious parties within the coalition. Together we demanded to have a letter from Secretary Clinton that would reaffirm that this would be the final extension of the freeze, and she was unwilling to issue a statement. The negotiation failed, and we were able to avoid the second extension. However, all the pressure that was put on the prime minister and the government had a chilling effect on Israel: Even if there is no official freeze the government cannot move forward because they're worried about the reaction in the United States. Even though there is no freeze today, the amount of units being built in Judea and Samaria and in parts of Jerusalem that were liberated in 1967 is not as high as it should be—that cooling effect is working.

We are not the problem, and the prime minister knows this, and Israelis know it. Prime Minister Netanyahu put the freeze in place to show the United States that Israel was listening to their concerns and to show goodwill, but it did not have the desired effect. By adopting the freeze, we were going back to the failed idea of "land for peace."

It was an ideological mistake because after the disengagement from Gaza the Israelis realized that the land-for-peace approach would never work. When we went out of Gaza we had to remove cemeteries and synagogues. We did not receive peace in exchange for this; we received missiles flying into major parts of Israel. Land for peace is an ideology and slogan of the left that has nothing to do with reality or positive outcomes. There is a large Arab city a few miles from my house and we have mixed cities of Arabs and Jews living peacefully in Israel. But for so many Palestinians and for many Americans and Westerners, the only way to achieve peace is to remove Jews. We are blamed in courts and media with "occupation," but look at the map and you will see that just under 3 percent of the land in Judea and Samaria is "occupied" by Jewish homes. I wish it was 90 percent.

When Vice President Biden visited Jerusalem in March 2010, the regional housing committee of the city approved a few units to be built in the northern part of the city in a neighborhood called Ramat Shlomo. It is an Orthodox neighborhood that is not under dispute, a fact that may have been missed by the U.S. administration. It was not done on purpose to embarrass him; the committee meets each month to approve projects. Israel's interior minister, Eli Yishai, who heads a religious party in Netanyahu's governing coalition, said the timing of the plan's approval was coincidental. "There was certainly no intention to provoke anyone and certainly not to come along and hurt the vice-president of the United States," Yishai told a reporter.

However, the U.S. reaction was very aggressive—the United States saw the approval as some sort of purposeful action against the peace process, and they manufactured a "crisis" out of it. Where else in the world does a sovereign nation require international approval in order to construct homes for its citizens in their own capital? The building approval was criticized by the State Department and denounced by the Palestinian Authority. "Unilateral action of this kind works against our efforts to get folks back to the table, makes it all more difficult," State Department spokeswoman Victoria Nuland said in Washington. "We think the best path forward is direct negotiations, so that the parties can agree together on an outcome that realizes the aspirations of both parties for Jerusalem."[70]

The same night as the vice president was scheduled to have a dinner with Prime Minister Netanyahu, the news broke out and it became an international incident. "The substance and timing of the announcement, particularly with the launching of proximity talks, is precisely the kind of step that undermines the trust we need right now," Mr. Biden said when learning of the building. "We must build an atmosphere to support negotiations, not complicate them," he added, warning that "unilateral action taken by either party cannot prejudge the outcome of negotiations."[71] As the news broke I was in a private meeting with the prime minister on other issues, discussing the compensation for families who could not build in Judea and Samaria because of the freeze and creating a formula for how we could do this quickly. After all, these were private buildings, not government buildings. The prime minister immediately canceled all other meetings and dealt with this artificial crisis by trying to explain that the building was not a provocation. Vice President Biden's remarks were in stark contrast to previous administrations' attitudes, since the building was occurring in a completely Jewish neighborhood and it is something that has been going on since 1967. The lesson from this incident is that the Americans quickly forgot about the freeze in Judea and Samaria and demanded an extension of the freeze into Jerusalem.

THE ASSAULTS CONTINUE

Discomforting behavior continues to come from the White House, which makes Israelis wonder whether the United States is really on our side—and strengthens the case that we must be confident to take matters, when necessary, into our own hands despite world or U.S. opinion. For example, in March 2012, leaks about Iran's nuclear program and the possibility of an Israeli military strike against it seemed to have originated from the Obama administration as part of an effort to pressure Israel not to bomb Iran, and for Iran to reach a compromise in nuclear talks. Specifically, a March 28, 2012, story in *Foreign Policy,* "Israel's Secret Staging Ground," reported that Israel might intend to use Azerbaijan as a base of operations in the event of an attack on Iranian nuclear facilities. The reporter noted that he had spoken to high-level sources within the Obama administration. The story was picked up widely in the press.

In 2011, a bill came under consideration in the Knesset that would limit foreign government funding of nongovernmental organizations (NGOs) that work toward de-legitimizing Israel. In April 2011, U.S. ambassador Dan Shapiro warned Israel that the bill limits the free speech rights of those who disagree with the government.[72] The proposed legislation on foreign government funding, in which I am intimately involved, is discussed at length in the next section of this chapter. But in short, why should Israel allow foreign governments to fund 23 NGOs? While we cannot prevent governments from funding NGOs, Israel can put limitations and regulations on the NGOs themselves that use that funding for political activities. In fact, these organizations receive more than 70 percent of their budgets from mainly European governments that *actively oppose* the policies of the democratically elected government of Israel. Would Americans not be disturbed if foreign governments were funding organizations that were working to de-legitimize America? More importantly, *why would the U.S. government want to help fund such activity in the first place?* This has absolutely zero to do with free speech or silencing opponents—people can and do voice their dissenting opinions every day in

Israel and private people can give money to these organizations if they choose to. That is not what the bill is about, and Mr. Shapiro as well as Secretary of State Hillary Clinton, who has also criticized it, should know this or read the bill more carefully. And lest you think that Israel is trying to do what the Egyptian government is trying to do with its arrest of NGO workers in that country, please think twice. The difference is, of course, that Israel has arrested or detained no one and has no plans to do so. Moreover, our argument is over foreign government funding of NGOs, not the very existence of such groups in Israel, which we accept.

In another instance, U.S. secretary of state Hillary Clinton had expressed shock at Israel's unfair treatment of women during a closed-door session in Washington in April 2011. I had to read the report twice before I believed it. In her defense, it may have been an off-the-cuff remark that the media blew out of proportion. It certainly happens. However, whether it was meant as a serious comment or not, it betrays a sense of misunderstanding about Israelis, and she should be careful not to generalize about an entire society based on a couple of isolated incidents. As examples, she mentioned some cases of IDF (Israeli Defense Forces) soldiers leaving during performances of female singers, and the fact that females sit in the back of buses in certain places in Israel. Clinton said that some of these phenomena reminded her of Iran.[73] It was almost as if Secretary Clinton was saying that Israel places as little value on human rights as Iran, one of the most repressive regimes in the world. In Iran, it is still possible for a woman to be found guilty of "bad hijab"—exposure of any part of the body other than hands and face—and if so, she could be subject to punishment of up to 70 lashes or imprisonment.[74] The legal age of arranged marriage for a girl is thirteen, and married girls are barred from attending regular schools. Segregation of sexes is the law in *all* public places. The Iranian judiciary implements Islamic penal code on both men and women, which includes, among other punishments, stoning, amputations, and flogging, which are considered to be torture under international law.[75]

In contrast, Secretary Clinton should remember that major parties are led by women in Israel, and the head of our Supreme Court was a woman. Israel is the only state in the Middle East that gives women full rights and full opportunities. Mrs. Clinton knows this of course—her own run for president might have even been in part inspired by Golda Meir, who was elected prime minister of Israel in 1969, becoming the world's second elected female state leader in modern times.

I do want to comment on the issues Secretary Clinton raises. As far as IDF soldiers are concerned, this issue began when IDF cadet Yoel Glickman was dismissed from an officers' course after refusing to listen to a female soldier sing during a military event. Cadet Glickman is in the Nahal Haredi regiment, and is Orthodox; he believes that listening to women sing is against religious law. The army, in fact, found a reasonable solution to the issue: When there is an official ceremony, soldiers must sit and listen to women singing as part of the event. However, they do not have to participate in leisure activities when singing by women is involved.[76]

In the section of Israel, and in Jerusalem in particular, where the bus incidents she referred to take place, some observe Orthodox code, which sometimes means separate seating for men and women. Perhaps this is not right, and extremists who believe this are part of a very small minority in Israel. I, myself, condemn the separation, instigated by extreme Haredim. However, it is by no means a cause for concern for women's rights in Israel. Israel works hard to accommodate religious people, and small extreme groups can make this difficult. We try to work through these challenges as any democratic nation would. Secretary Clinton knows this and knows better.

In December 2012 U.S. defense secretary Leon Panetta demanded that Israel "just get to the damn table" to negotiate with the Palestinians and "mend fences" with Turkey, Egypt, and other Islamist regimes by "performing more gestures"—the code for more concessions. The deeper meaning to his outrage is that Israel singularly stands in the way of peace because of a refusal to negotiate and because it antagonizes its neighbors with hostile overtures. Mr. Panetta conveniently forgets it was the Palestinian Authority that walked away from peace talks. And Israel's "gestures" or concessions include the aforementioned ten-month construction freeze, which held the promise of getting Palestinians back to the table. It did not. As far as our other neighbors are concerned, it's hard to know exactly what Panetta is talking about. Radical Islamists, whose stated foreign policies are hostile to Israel, influence the new governments in both Turkey and Egypt. Turkey's prime minister Recep Tayyip Erdogan has threatened to increase naval surveillance patrols of the eastern Mediterranean Sea, freeze defense trade with Israel, and allow Turkish gunboats to accompany Turkish "humanitarian" vessels—that is, illegal flotillas—the next time they set sail for Gaza. These are just a few examples of the prime minister's animosity toward Israel.[77] Egypt's Arab Spring resulted in an attack on the Egyptian Israeli Embassy, increased violence in the Sinai, and a loosening of borders that allows Hamas easier access to weapons.

Howard Gutman, U.S. ambassador in Belgium, blamed Israel for anti-Semitism at a conference in Brussels.[78] He basically said that Muslim anti-Semitism was understandable and tolerable (unlike traditional anti-Semitism)—and Israel's fault. He also argued, with a straight face, that an Israeli-Palestinian peace treaty would significantly diminish Muslim anti-Semitism while speaking in front of the same Jewish conference on anti-Semitism organized by the European Jewish Union (EJU).

If there were no Israel, there would still be anti-Semitism, as there was before the State was created. The Palestinians would be no happier since they are raised on hatred. The Middle East would be no more peaceful—the regions would simply revert to infighting. It is a fight of cultures that is not about land or where borders will be drawn—both convenient ruses. The idea of an Israel-free utopia is a ridiculous ideologically driven fantasy. In fact, well before there were any "Palestinians," in 1929, Arab mobs murdered more than one hundred Jews, the majority of them in Hebron, an ancient community where Jews had lived among Arabs peacefully for centuries. The Mufti of Jerusalem enthusiastically urged his ally Hitler to wipe out European Jews during World War II, before the State of Israel was established, while the Mufti promised to do the same for Jews in the Middle East.[79] Ambassador Gutman needs to brush up on his history.

These U.S. incidents all may seem like small examples, and as such are easily trivialized and dismissed. But taken together they create a picture in which the Obama administration has a dim view of Israel. Such interactions chip away at an important relationship and also undermine our trust in the United States.

THE IDEOLOGICAL WAR ON ISRAEL

There is another thread that Israel is forced to contend with, one that is more existential and gaining in currency. That is, the growing acceptance in the United States and abroad of a left-wing, so-called progressive position on Israel with a one-sided view of Palestinian aspirations.

I define the progressive left as those who believe in a large centralized government, promote the idea that socioeconomic and racial classes are naturally at odds with one another, believe in privileged victim groups and oppressors and oppressed in nearly every social and political situation, hold that fairness and equality are conditions that can be legislated by government, and often promote the idea of a one-world government. I define the hard right as people who hold extreme nationalist, xenophobic, religious fundamentalist, or reactionary views. Both groups often believe that free speech should be curtailed according to their ideologies.

Anti-Israeli ideology started on college campuses in the United States in the 1960s and 1970s, and has now seeped into significant segments of the American public. It has become popular for the left to blame Israel for many of the ills and violence in the Middle East—particularly in the press and academia, in both the United States and Israel. It shows not only a commitment to a deeply flawed ideology but a troubling misunderstanding of what is really happening in the region. Such thought has also found fertile ground in Europe; the question "Why do we even have to care what happens to Israel?" has become almost mainstream in some countries. This seems almost benign until you understand that according to a European Union poll, almost 60 percent of the Europeans surveyed believed Israel was more dangerous than North Korea, Iran, Iraq, and Afghanistan.[80] It is absolutely astounding that Israel, a full democracy, is considered more dangerous than expressly hostile regimes such as Iran and North Korea. In a worldwide BBC poll, Israel and Iran tied for first place as the nation with the most negative influence.[81] As a result of this kind of thinking, many in the West have turned a blind eye to the threats that are directed not only at Israel but, ironically, at themselves as well.

How is it that a nation that was created only three years after the Holocaust and with most of the world's approval became such a pariah state in the minds of so many? In the past, opposition was on the far right; however, for the last few decades it has been on the far left that we see the worst Israel bashers. As opposed to the extreme right, the extreme left is welcomed and even looked up to and lauded by the mainstream West, particularly in Europe, and in many sectors of the United States. The extreme left has penetrated media, university faculty, the political world, and even the Christian church in America and abroad.

Why does the left have such a disconnect when it comes to Israel? First, it's a safe and easy way to express disgust with America. The left likes to view Israel as an outpost of colonialism. Israel is also considered a basically Western, modern nation—and for this we can be judged by a Western left that tends to romanticize non-Western nations for their indigenous superiority—ironic given that Jews are the indigenous people of Israel. That is, Jews have lived in this land continuously from the time of its original conquest by Joshua more than 3,200 years ago until the present day, despite the fact that Jews have not always been in political control of the land, nor have they always been the majority population. Nonetheless, Israel is not protected by cultural relativism that is extended on a regular basis to Islamists. There is no right or wrong for indigenous people, according to the cultural relativist. Cultural relativism values and respects most cultural and religious practices; however, Christianity and Judaism are often exceptions to this rule. For instance, criticizing Islam is now a punishable offense in several European countries, including Norway and Denmark.[82] Cultural relativism asserts that the rights of women and girls, for example, are relative to their cultures and religions. As a result, cultural relativism supports and emboldens sexual apartheid and violence against women in Islamic communities and societies because such violence is a part of their culture and religion,[83] whereas the same acts of violence would be rightly condemned in Western societies. The left is also uncomfortable with religious Israelis who make biblical connections to the land, something I discuss at length in the last section of this book.

Amazingly, those who see themselves as members of the "progressive" left all too often champion the undemocratic, the homophobic, the misogynist, the racist, and the extreme religious policies of Islamists over the only democracy in the Middle East. This hostility toward Israel was not always the case, as the far left initially welcomed and embraced the new Jewish State. In 1948, a cultural hero of the American left, the African American folk singer Paul Robeson, electrified the crowd at a gala concert in Moscow with his rendition of a Yiddish partisan fighter song. The crowd was in an ecstatic mood because of the support the Soviet Union offered the new State of Israel. At that time many on the left who were expressly anti-American saw Israel as a Bolshevik creation, due to the ideologies of many of the "founding fathers" of Israel.

There was no greater endorsement of Zionism than that given by the Soviet delegate Andrei Gromyko, who in his famous speech to the U.N. General Assembly on May 14, 1947 (a full year before the Israeli declaration of statehood), asserted the right of "the Jews of the whole world to the creation of a state of their own," declaring, "It would be unjust not to take account of this fact and to deny the Jewish People the right to realize such aspirations." Israel was expected to be at the forefront of the anti-colonialist project when the British and French Empires were finally beginning to fall. Many who sympathized with the Soviet Union expected Israel to become a satellite of communism in the Middle East. Israel's struggle against the marauding Arabs was seen as a heroic stand and massive amounts of sympathy were extended to the plucky little nation.

This all changed after a couple of decades as Israel showed in 1967 that it could push back all the neighboring Arab nations in just six days. Although this brought astonishment and respect to

Israel in the short term, in the long term, Israel was now seen as the powerful oppressor and the Arabs became the weak victim. It is natural for people to support the seemingly defenseless against the seemingly strong. No doubt Israelis are tough, but another quick look at a map of the region tells you why this is a necessity. The extreme left had already grown to love groups like the PLO in the seventies and eighties, and saw them as "freedom-fighters." In 1977, British actress Vanessa Redgrave filmed a documentary titled *The Palestinians* that showed her in a PLO training camp, dancing as she waved a rifle over her head. In 1978, while accepting an Oscar, Redgrave railed at the "Zionist hoodlums." Amazingly enough, Redgrave became a UNICEF Goodwill ambassador even while espousing support and love for such figures as Yasser Arafat and Fidel Castro.

The First Intifada brought these views into the mainstream. The singular image of a small child in the shadow of a tank played nicely in the living rooms of armchair liberals. In reference to this image, the BBC website includes a line about the First Intifada: "it was the stone-throwing demonstrations against the heavily-armed occupation troops that captured international attention."[84] Although the BBC declared that "there was heavy loss of life among Palestinian civilians," there was no mention of any Israeli casualties. Organizations like the United Nations paint similar pictures. On December 22, 1987, the U.N. Security Council passed Resolution 605, which "strongly deplored" Israeli policies in the occupied territories that were seen to violate Palestinian human rights, "in particular, opening fire of the Israeli army, resulting in the killing and wounding of defenseless Palestinian civilians."

The United Nations has been at the forefront of de-legitimizing a state that it helped legally found. Ever since the United Nations was split into regional bodies, Israel has become the scapegoat for all the world's ills, according to this organization. Starting in the mid-1970s, an Arab–Soviet–third world bloc formed what amounted to a pro-PLO lobby at the United Nations. This was particularly true in the General Assembly, where these countries, nearly all dictatorships or autocracies, frequently voted together to pass resolutions attacking Israel and supporting the PLO. This culminated in the notorious General Assembly Resolution 3379, which slandered Zionism by branding it as a form of racism. Of all the forms of self-determination in the world, only the Jewish one was racist, according to the world body.

If anyone was in any doubt that these were more than words to terrorists, Chaim Herzog, an ambassador to the United Nations, said that the PLO used frequent U.N. condemnations of Israel as justification for terrorist attacks. Herzog further noted that the United Nations developed an Alice in Wonderland perspective on Israel. "In the UN building . . . she would only have to wear a Star of David in order to hear the imperious 'Off with her head' at every turn."[85]

The most egregious example of how the United Nations is used by those who oppose Israel is the Human Rights Council (HRC). The HRC was established in 2006 to replace the Commission on Human Rights, which had become farcical for allowing the worst human rights violators to participate in deliberations and to approve a steady stream of one-sided condemnations of Israel. After only a few months of operation, however, it became obvious the new council was worse than the original. Of the 47 members, 17 are members of the Organization of the Islamic Conference, and repressive dictatorships such as China and Cuba are also members.[86]

Western nations were at pains to focus the council's attention on the genocide in Darfur because the majority of members chose instead to produce a series of reports criticizing Israel.

For example, the council did not criticize Hezbollah for attacking Israel, kidnapping its soldiers, indiscriminately firing missiles at Israel, or using Lebanese civilians as shields. Instead, it condemned Israel for "violations of human rights and breaches of international humanitarian law in Lebanon."[87] When a report was produced in October 2006 that criticized both Hezbollah and Israel, Muslim members of the council rejected it.[88]

This has become a source of embarrassment to many at the United Nations. U.N. secretary-general Kofi Annan admitted at the opening of the 61st General Assembly on September 20, 2006, that Israel is often unfairly judged at the United Nations. "On one side, supporters of Israel feel that it is harshly judged by standards that are not applied to its enemies," he said. "And too often this is true, particularly in some UN bodies."[89] However, too many people consider U.N. resolutions and statements as sacrosanct and take them at face value without question.

The United Nations has become so permeated with hatred that the prejudice does not end with Israel but all too often extends to all Jews. "The Talmud says that if a Jew does not drink every year the blood of a non-Jewish man, he will be damned for eternity," Saudi Arabian delegate Marouf al-Dawalibi said before the 1984 U.N. Human Rights Commission conference on religious tolerance.[90] The Syrian ambassador made a similar remark at a 1991 meeting, insisting Jews killed Christian children to use their blood to make matzot.[91]

Although anti-Semitism plays a major role in the hate directed at Israel, it is definitely not the whole story. It has become impossible for the rational Western mind to understand how a person becomes a suicide bomber and craves death. This Western mind superimposes his or her viewpoint and outlook onto the situation and surmises that it must take intense oppression to make a person kill himself or herself while murdering complete strangers. In the Arab world, there is a cult of the suicide bomber. There is no higher calling than strapping a bomb around the waist or chest. Once the deed is done, the bombers become martyrs who are worshipped, and their photographs and images are plastered on walls in homes and in public squares. As Murad Tawalbi, a failed Palestinian suicide bomber, related in an interview in 2003, "I was very happy. I was waiting for the time to come. I was counting the seconds before I went down. I felt very calm, as if nothing were happening. When I put on the belt of explosives, it felt like it was nothing at all. My brother put it on me, and I was watching him, looking for tears in his eyes, but there weren't any. He was smiling, and that encouraged me more."[92]

Findings have shown many times that terrorists, far from being oppressed, uneducated, and underprivileged, are more likely to be from well-educated, middle-class backgrounds. At Princeton University, economist Alan Krueger has studied not only suicide bombers but also the views of the Palestinian public on terror attacks aimed at Israelis. Again, surveys found no link between poverty and illiteracy and support for terror.

Many who do not consider themselves anti-Semites nevertheless hold anti-Semitic views. According to the European Monitoring Centre on Racism and Xenophobia (EUMC), there are several ways that anti-Semitism can manifest itself toward Israel:

1. Denying the Jewish people their right to self-determination, e.g., by claiming that the existence of a State of Israel is a racist endeavor.
2. Applying double standards by requiring of it a behavior not expected or demanded of any other democratic nation.

3. Drawing comparisons of contemporary Israeli policy to that of the Nazis.[93]

By these standards it would appear that most of the world holds anti-Semitic views. This would even include mainstream Western leaders such as the late Swedish prime minister Olof Palme and the late Greek prime minister Andreas Papandreou, both of whom have compared Israelis with the Nazis.[94] Recently, many have compared Israel to the apartheid regime in South Africa in the hope of implementing a successful boycott, as was used there. The comparison to apartheid South Africa fits squarely within the EUMC definition of anti-Semitism by suggesting that the State of Israel is a racist endeavor. People who have used this comparison include former American president Jimmy Carter, Iranian foreign minister Ali Akbar Salehi, Cuban deputy foreign minister Abelardo Moreno, and Saudi prince Turki bin Mohammed bin Saud Al-Kabeer.[95] The comparison has also been made by numerous college professors, including Nada Elia, Ph.D., who currently teaches global and gender studies at Antioch University–Seattle[96]; Stephen Shalom of political science at William Paterson University; and Jeff Goodwin, a professor of sociology at New York University. In addition, the list includes world-renowned linguist and U.S. foreign policy critic Noam Chomsky,[97] as well as members of Israel Apartheid Week, an organization active on American and European college campuses that aims "to educate people about the nature of Israel as an apartheid system"[98]; along with many "average" Americans and Europeans whom I have met in my travels who, frankly, don't know any better.

Professor Gideon Shimoni explains the underlying differences between those who use this term and those who don't. "Apartheid has become one of the world's most potent defamatory code-words. Hence those who a-priori seek fatally to stigmatize Israel grasp it with alacrity as a weapon in the struggle to end its existence as a Jewish state. In a sense, the Israel=apartheid fallacy can serve as a litmus test for distinguishing between those who are hostile to Israel's very existence and those who are conscientious critics of the policies and actions of Israel's governments and public," Shimoni said.[99]

The fact remains that through a combination of self-delusion, anti-Semitism, and a left-wing bias in the media, academia, and politics, the West has yet to grasp that Israel is not the oppressor. If people do not receive the correct information, how can they construct informed opinions? Israel has become a pariah state because of these factors and it is not because of any occupation and oppression. Independent human rights organizations consistently find that Israel has a very good human rights record.

UNIVERSITY JIHAD

According to the Anti-Defamation League, Al-Awda (the Palestine Right to Return Coalition) is an organization that opposes Israel's right to exist; supports groups on the U.S. State Department's list of foreign terrorist organizations, including Hamas and Hezbollah; and organizes many rallies and demonstrations to demonize Israel. On February 13, 2011, Al-Awda held its fifth Al-Awda West Coast Regional Conference in the La Mesa Community Center in San Diego, California. Investigative journalist Lee Kaplan attended the meeting and wrote an article that raised several troubling issues for anyone concerned about the safety of Jewish students on California campuses.

In October 2011, Students for Justice in Palestine (SJP) held a three-day training program on the Columbia University campus in New York City. According to one report on the event, the Muslim Brotherhood offers support to student organizations like SJP and the Muslim Student Association (MSA).[100] By the way, the first stage of the Muslim Brotherhood's three-stage blueprint for covert jihad, written in the early 1920s, calls for the spread of the Islamic message through propaganda, media, confrontation, and character assassination of opponents, and the training of messengers of Islam in the form of professors and lecturers to reach schools, mosques, and public facilities. Islamists have found that invading Western culture through its educational institutions is an extremely effective strategy to spread the word of Allah. One of the main attractions at the conference was the rapper Immortal Technique, who, according to the National Conference on Jewish Affairs (NCJA), is an entertainer "who extols and incites violence and criminality, spews brutal anti-American vitriol, and is a condemner of Israel . . . and a fan of the Nation of Islam, among other repellent views."[101]

The event organizers hoped to raise $30,000 in preparation for the 2012 national campus event called Israel Apartheid Week, which has been held the past seven years in February or March. The annual series of university lectures and rallies began in Toronto in 2005 and has since spread to campuses in 55 cities. The event promotes boycott, divestment, and sanctions against Israel. Let's just clarify for a moment that South African apartheid was a legal system of discrimination based on race, with a minority white Afrikaner community imposing severe inequalities and patterns of separation upon the black majority within the borders of the South African nation. The issue in Israel is political-national. At its heart are claims to the land between the Jordan River and the Mediterranean Sea. This is a vastly different scenario from the South African one.

At any rate, when one enters the SJP website you are greeted by the message, "America's college students are at the cutting edge of the global free Palestine movement in the US and across the globe and they are making a difference." And of course there is the requisite endorsement from Noam Chomsky there, as well: "SJP has done fine work mobilizing such forces and the prospects for significant achievement are very real."

Despite NCJA's pleas to Columbia to cancel the event, it went forward as planned. SJP is not the only group on campus that promotes a one-sided view of Israeli-Palestinian relations and encourages an anti-Zionist viewpoint. At the University of California, Berkeley, students have been treated to guerrilla theater, including reenactments of IDF soldiers mowing down Palestinians.[102]

Members of the UC Berkeley SJP have harassed and committed acts of physical aggression against Jewish students and disrupted Jewish student events. SJP advocates economic sanctions against Israel, and its chapters were responsible for divestment at Hampshire College, a small private college in Amherst, Massachusetts, and the University of Rochester, as well as the most recent, widely publicized failed attempt at UC Berkeley.[103]

At Boston College, pro-Palestinian sentiment is so deeply embedded that Professor Eve Spangler felt free to describe Palestinian terrorists (she calls them "dissidents") as possessing "courage and wisdom" in the syllabus for her class "Social Justice in Israel/Palestine." Furthermore, part of the requirement of the class is to leave it as an activist for Palestine: "The project that students are asked to design (in the seminar) and to implement (upon their return) should allow students to test their capacity for using their education to do good in the world."[104]

The steady drumbeat of anti-Israel propaganda on campus has a cumulative impact on the overall image of Israel. It also means

Jewish students and their supporters are not always prepared for what they find at college, especially in the classroom, where anti-Israel faculty have been entrenched for some time. More than that, the intimidation and harassment of Jewish students on campuses is indefensible and plays no part in the debate on Middle East policy. Unfortunately, such events happen regularly on college campuses in the United States and elsewhere—both in and out of the classroom. According to the FBI's statistics for 2010, 71.9 percent of all religiously motivated hate crimes in America were directed at Jews, a truly frightening statistic, especially since Jews make up only around 1.7 percent of the total population in the United States.[105]

It's not that I am averse to criticism of the State of Israel. On the contrary, I actively welcome a healthy debate on the subject of Israel and the Middle East. It is a legitimate and crucial part of civil discourse. However, criticism that demonizes Israel by incorporating traditional anti-Semitic stereotypes or by comparing Israel's leaders to Nazis or practitioners of apartheid does cross the line into anti-Semitism. Moreover, these kinds of arguments do nothing to expand the conversation; indeed they are meant specifically to shut down dissenters. Joseph Massad, assistant professor of modern Arab politics and intellectual history in the Department of Middle Eastern Languages and Cultures (MEALAC) at Columbia University, describes himself as a "Palestinian-Jordanian," routinely condemns Israel as a "racist state," and has called for its destruction. In April 2002, for instance, he delivered a public lecture wherein he castigated Israel as "a Jewish supremacist and racist state," adding that "[e]very racist state should be destroyed." One month earlier, Massad had insisted that the "Jewish state is a racist state that does not have the right to exist."[106]

Kent State history professor Julio Pino shouted "Death to Israel" at a public lecture by former Israeli diplomat Ishmael Khaldi. Pino asked Khaldi how Israel could justify providing aid to countries such as Turkey with "blood money" from the deaths of Palestinians, according to the student website. "Is this what that professor is telling you?" Khaldi asked after Pino stormed out of the room. "It is my responsibility to tell you the truth and build relationships."[107] A native of Cuba and convert to Islam, Pino has fueled the fire of anti-Israel sentiment on campus for several years. In 2002, for example, he wrote a column in the *Daily Kent Stater* eulogizing an 18-year-old Palestinian suicide bomber. There are dozens more examples of such professors, from obscure players like Pino, who have tenure in history, English, and other departments in colleges and universities from coast to coast, to rock star–level individuals like Noam Chomsky, who command large audiences and much public attention.

Tens of millions of dollars, most of it from the Middle East, have been channeled to American universities over the years to fund curricula on the Middle East.[108] Almost none of that funding has gone toward developing courses on Israel. According to a study done by the Israel on Campus Coalition, there are 125 Middle East studies programs in American institutions. The Department of Education funds 14 Middle East centers and nearly 100 student fellowships at a cost of $4 million per year.[109] Between 1986 and 2007, Arabs spent $300 million in universities in the United States and invested millions in the United Kingdom, where students are being radicalized.[110] There needs to be an investment in people, not just buildings, from the other side, so that professors and scholars can help encourage counter-activities between Christian and Jewish students so those who support Israel feel strong enough to speak out.

It's almost impossible to fight anti-Israeli programs and professors because the discussion will always come down to free speech, and that's a battle you'll always lose. The only way to make progress is by ensuring there is a balance of professors teaching Israeli history—and not only from a left-wing ideological viewpoint. I'm not saying that Israeli history should be taught without criticism, but from multiple points of view. My philosophy is to give students the opportunity to learn the facts about Israel from objective professors. There are organizations that have made important headway on campuses and this work must continue. For instance, StandWithUs is an international, nonprofit organization dedicated to informing the public about Israel and to combating the extremism and anti-Semitism that often distorts the issues. They offer support to people around the world who want to educate their own local campuses.

The American-Israeli Cooperative Enterprise (AICE) brings visiting Israeli professors to colleges and universities and in the past years has brought 90 such scholars to campuses across the United States. The professors can make and have made a big difference by bringing different perspectives and resources to students. Israeli studies should also be on par with other disciplines so students study Israeli history the same way they study French history or American history, so it's not just about conflict. Students should also learn about culture, history, and politics. AICE brings in professors who teach film, literature, music, sociology, and science.

There has been some progress made in bringing more Israeli scholars to schools. There used to be only two centers for Israeli studies in the United States, at NYU and Brandeis. But now there are several more, including at Emory University, American University, and UCLA. San Francisco State, one of the most anti-Semitic campuses in the country, has an Israeli studies program with an endowed chair, the Goldman Chair. The same has happened at Berkeley, which has had a visiting Israeli professor for two years. This will help to change the complexion of campus life because Berkeley is ground zero for political activism and a great deal of anti-Israeli rhetoric—for example, Berkeley was in the forefront of fighting for the divestment resolution. The program is run through its law school, which is significant in many ways. For one thing, Berkeley is one of the top law schools in the world and the dean, who was one of Obama's transition advisors, supported the visiting professorship program. They will grow the program and this will have a ripple effect across the country in terms of adding such programs to curricula at other colleges. Obviously this is a beginning, and more work needs to be done.

MEDIA BIAS

For years the State of Israel has suffered from the David vs. Goliath concept, which is accurate—except the media often has this concept backward. I could fill this book with one example after another of how the media twists reporting on Israel and the Israeli-Palestinian conflict. It's easier and more effective to relate concepts about distance and size, such as the fact that Israel is the size of New Jersey, and almost completely surrounded by much larger countries with huge swaths of land and bigger populations who would like to see it destroyed (see Appendix E). Still, the media worldwide writes of the "Jewish settlements" and "West Bank" as key conflicts between the Arabs and Israel. Why aren't Jordan and Egypt ever asked to give up land to accommodate the Palestinian population? Blaming Israel for the problems of the Middle East is like blaming a flea for a pit bull's aggressive behavior.

One of the problems is that journalists graduate from the schools I just discussed. It's worth reviewing some recent lapses of journalistic coverage. Why? Because what some of the American press reports and how they report it has a profound effect on how Americans view Israel, which puts us both in danger. Allowing American reporters to frame the debate in a way that continuously paints Israel as a powerful aggressor puts a wedge in the fault line that already exists between the two parties. The real threat in the region is not coming from Israel but from Islamic extremists, radicalized terrorists and their supporters and appeasers who will never be satisfied, even if Israel is driven into the sea. It was one of the lessons learned on September 11, 2001—it doesn't matter if you ignore the extremists, they will come and find you.

In one alarming example of what has become a string of blame-the-victim reporting, the September 11, 2011, issue of the *New York Times* ran a front-page story placing most of the blame on Israel for the Cairo Embassy takeover that occurred the day before. This is incredible since the writer was referring to two events. The first, Israeli troops who killed five Egyptian policemen while pursuing a group of Palestinian gunmen who had crossed into Israel from Egypt's Sinai Peninsula and killed eight Israelis. The second, Israel's refusal to apologize for the 2010 raid on a blockade-running Turkish ship, in which nine violent Turkish extremists were killed when they brutally attacked Israeli commandos boarding the ship. Some Israeli reporters do take the same blame-the-victim tack. The story quotes Israeli newspapers that believe Prime Minister Netanyahu was partly to blame for the Cairo takeover because he had not done anything to mitigate the fallout from these two events. However, Israel does not apologize for actions it deems defensive, and such was the case with both of these situations.

Not to be outdone by the *Times,* the *Washington Post,* in an October 31, 2011, article about a weekend of rocket attacks from Hamas-controlled Gaza and Israeli counter-strikes, says that the firefight was Israel's fault because it allegedly fired the first shot. Aside from that not being the case, the headline of the *Post*'s web story is unsurprisingly telling: "Israeli airstrike kills militant in fresh Gaza violence." The report said that the Israeli army had targeted militants preparing to fire long-range rockets into Israel—meaning that it was a preemptive strike and that Islamic Jihad was only reacting to an Israeli breach of a cease-fire agreement.

This is not true. A few days before, on October 26, Islamic Jihad terrorists launched a homemade GRAD rocket, made with materials from Iran, toward Ashdod, a major town in southern Israel. According to reports, one missile landed about 1,200 meters from a large, populated apartment building. An elementary school suffered a direct hit, but was empty at the time. Another missile hit a house in a village immediately east of Ashdod, causing extensive damage and injuring one person. A second barrage of four GRAD missiles crashed into an apartment building parking lot. Numerous people were injured and many suffered from shock and had to be treated, but miraculously no one was killed—perhaps this is the reason the reporter failed to mention this earlier attack. However, it was the first unprovoked cross-border attack since the prisoner swap between Israel and Hamas that freed Israeli Sergeant Gilad Shalit from five years of Hamas captivity in exchange for the release of more than 1,000 Palestinian terrorists and criminals. Israeli military intelligence uncovered the identity of the five Islamic Jihad terrorists who were responsible for the attack on Ashdod. Three days later, the army was able to get them in their sights as they prepared to fire a rocket.

IDEOLOGY BOUGHT WITH EUROS

Many nongovernmental organizations (NGOs) call themselves "the guardians of human rights" as a way to ease their conscience, such as Breaking the Silence[111] and B'Tselem.[112] But foreign governments that are clear in their anti-Israel policies financially support extreme left-wing anti-Israeli organizations. These vitriolic groups have been working for years against the Israel Defense Forces and the Israeli government. In many other democracies, including ones that fund these organizations, these groups would have to deal with legal action—not to mention widespread public outcry at their actions.

As much as radical NGOs try to claim that their actions are advancing the cause of peace, some of their activities, such as those coming from Peace Now,[113] are actually pushing this dream further and further away. These campaigns don't hold back from using any method available to them—they de-legitimize the State of Israel, attempt to limit our options, and deter us from defending ourselves. Moreover, the actions by these organizations are doing irreparable damage to Israel's interests overseas, damage that no amount of effort by our dedicated diplomats and supporters will be able to rectify. Many people argue that we incite against organizations that deal only with human rights issues and do not get involved politically whatsoever and when those governments are asked about political intervention in our democracy, they say they only support humanitarian, educational, and nonpolitical activities. But it has proven to be the opposite, as evidenced in the protocols of these organizations:

1. Protocol from the Commission for the Middle East
    Region of the European Council—1999
        The funding of the organization Peace Now, intended
    to promote an educational campaign for peace. The

campaign will target a specific demographic, which is inherently against peace and votes for the Likud party. It is important to present this demographic the benefits of peace.

2. A copy of the contract signed between the European Union Council and the Israeli organization Keren Te'ena, which details the transfer of over 350,000 Euros intended to influence the opinions of immigrants (from the former Soviet Union), for a peace resolution that is based on territorial recognition and mutual land concession.
    This goal can be achieved by developing an educational program for the Russian-speaking community in order to create awareness on their perspective for a solution to the conflict. Such a program is vital in shifting the opinions of the Russian-speaking communities towards this peace plan.

While we recognize the importance of freedom of expression in our democratic society, we all know that reasonable limits must prevail—fair and reasonable rules of the game. How can we allow foreign governments to "buy ideologies" within Israel by paying out millions of Euros every year? We must understand that they have only one true goal—the end of legitimate Israeli sovereignty.

Those who question our obligation to investigate this noxious challenge must first ask themselves important questions. What right do these countries have to claim an interest in the internal social issues of our society? Why do they feel entitled to meddle in our most sensitive diplomatic and security decisions through devious, deceitful methods?

Can one imagine the Vatican allowing foreign groups to actively undermine their duly formulated policies? I don't object to private individuals funding certain projects, whether left or right, but it is outrageous when you see governments trying to change Israelis' way of thinking. Would the United States sit by idly while nongovernmental groups funded by foreign governments stalked and monitored their soldiers' every move during dangerous and complicated combat missions? Of course not. If anything, this type of behavior is routinely classified as "aiding and abetting" terrorist organizations, and its perpetrators usually face stern justice, including imprisonment and fines. This is a natural reaction from democratic nations, without even mentioning the draconian punishment meted out to terrorists and their facilitators in the not-so-enlightened justice systems of some of our less democratic neighbors.

It is inconceivable that a sovereign, enlightened state would allow governmental elements to play an active role in influencing the internal workings of its society. It is further unimaginable that rational and fair leadership would allow this phenomenon to fester and would not work diligently to uproot and put an end to such behavior. We should be proud, not embarrassed, to state that it is our responsibility as leaders to do the right thing for our country. We must never shy away from defending our citizens.

If these organizations do not come to the realization that they are being manipulated and taken advantage of by outside extremists in order to harm our state, then it is our duty to act decisively and legislate appropriately to protect our society. Just as we send our young men and women to the front lines to risk their lives for our state, we must embark on this "social war" of norms to protect our democracy and re-instill a sense of trust, confidence, and pride in our society.

It's worth mentioning again, as I did earlier, that our efforts to stop foreign governments from funding NGOs bent on destroying

Israel are not parallel to what happened in Egypt when the government there arrested several NGO workers for promoting democracy. Israel has not arrested anyone, nor have we detained any member of an NGO. We are working democratically, within a democratic system, to find a solution to an issue that actually could strike at the very core of our democracy and survival.

ISRAEL MUST DO BETTER

Because we are a democracy, our message changes with elections, new ideological trends, and the myriad voices that recede and advance. When there is a change of government, each new administration brings its own ideas, which they try to market to the people and win support. When the Likud's Yitzhak Shamir was the prime minister, he did not believe in negotiations with terrorist organizations, and that was the message. When Yitzhak Rabin and Shimon Peres of the Labor party were in power, it was a different message. It's very difficult to convince everyone to go along with the new message each time there is an election. Instead, we have to adapt to the changing scene and adopt new strategies to win the public relations (PR) war from wherever we sit.

As a proud Zionist and as a politician who understands how public perception works, I understand that Israel doesn't always see PR as a vital part of the war. The State of Israel places itself in real danger because of flawed public relations and communications work. In contrast, Hamas and Hezbollah are very practiced at engaging reporters and journalists, sharing meals and drinks with them, and ultimately, winning their favor. Both terror groups hire aggressive PR agencies to lobby on their behalf in the press and on the world stage. For instance, in 2009, Fenton Communications, an American New York City–based PR firm, signed two contracts with the Arab state of Qatar to develop an 18-month campaign for the Al Fakhoora project.[114] Although billed as an educational project, in my view its real aim is to essentially de-legitimize Israel by orchestrating an international anti-Israel campaign. There are numerous other examples of PR firms hired to put a positive spin on Arab terror groups. Israel should take a lesson from this and do the same.

The problem with Israel is that because we are a democracy with competing viewpoints, we do a poor job of framing the debate in a united way. For instance, Palestinians who throw rocks and Molotov cocktails and then are shot at are quite deceptively portrayed as victims in the media and elsewhere. But think about this—what would happen if a group of teenagers threw rocks, boulders, and homemade explosive devices at police and civilians in the streets of Los Angeles, New York, or Chicago? Would the police not deter them vigorously and perhaps with force? This is a simple argument that is quite logical and rational, but that is not often made by Israeli spokespeople.

The same kind of thing happens when private investors legally buy property in eastern Jerusalem and build homes for Jews. A quick Internet search reveals that media and governments worldwide see such construction as evidence of Jewish "occupation" and as a primary reason why there will never be peace in the Middle East. Instead, Israel could easily create a different message—again using logic: A Jewish person can buy a home legally, build it, and live anywhere in the world *except* Jerusalem? It's a question of shaping concepts and of speaking in terms and metaphors that the world can visualize, relate to, and understand.

During my studies at Hebrew University of Jerusalem, I, along with a few friends, formed an organization to support Jerusalem as the united capital of Israel. In 1997, one of the first activities we undertook was to participate in an action where a Jewish family moved into a legally purchased home in an area of eastern Jerusalem called Ras Al Amoud by Arabs and Maa'ale HaZeitim by Jews.

The home was in an Arab neighborhood and we eventually built a Jewish neighborhood, starting with that one house. There was a lot of pressure put on both Prime Minister Netanyahu and Jerusalem's mayor at the time, Ehud Olmert, to prevent us from moving in, but it was legally impossible to stop.

When we took possession of the house, for the first few days it was stoned by Arab mobs. My car, which was parked outside of the building, was completely destroyed. Surprisingly, when the security people called the police, located one mile away, they turned up only after a few hours had passed. Perhaps the delay in response was because the police thought we would leave if we believed they would not protect us. Then there started to be international pressure to leave. We conducted hundreds of worldwide media interviews at the home, all done with the recognizable Dome of the Rock as a backdrop. Reporters tried to editorialize that it was a so-called disputed Jewish area of Jerusalem, but viewers could clearly see the close proximity of this territory to the Jerusalem they recognized. The small house was eventually replaced with an apartment building. Today when I visit my friends who live in that beautiful neighborhood, I feel that we did the right thing: We stuck to our beliefs. It is a safe neighborhood with a vibrant Jewish community.

Another example of how we can do better winning the PR war is when Israel boarded a flotilla ship on May 31, 2010. While en route to Gaza, commandos from the IDF raided and seized the *Mavi Marmara* (the flotilla) after communicating clear warnings that a naval blockade of the Gaza area was in force. The

commandos were seemingly unprepared for the dozens of militant terrorists who swarmed around them wielding knives and
iron bars. A bloody battle took place; nine flotilla passengers were
killed in the melee, and at least seven IDF soldiers were wounded.
It was a major diplomatic debacle for the Israeli government. The
public responded, enraged, because initially it appeared that
Israeli soldiers were storming the ship violently—soldiers who, by
the way, were carrying paint guns, not actual weapons—and had
attacked first, which they did not.

Even if you believe, as I do, that Israel's actions in boarding
the flotilla were entirely justified, the way Israel handled the crisis
was a huge tactical and strategic fiasco. The boat received many
clear warnings not to enter Israel's sovereign space, and the boat
proceeded anyway. What's surprising about soldiers wanting to
stop foreigners from coming illegally onshore? Even if people are
"peaceful"—and the boat passengers weren't—does that mean
a peaceful group can take their own flotilla to Guantanamo Bay
or Canada or New York Harbor? And would media reports say
Canadian police were wrong to respond to a boatload of people who refused to stop when asked, and then attacked the police when they boarded the ship? Again, try taking a boat over to
Guantanamo Bay, or even Rikers Island in New York City and see
what the response would be.

The resulting coverage and Israel's hand-wringing and late-
to-the-game response did long-term damage to the Jewish State's
already badly bruised international reputation. The Gaza flotilla
was comprised of eight ships and about 800 participants. The
event wasn't organized by peaceful humanitarians with pure motivations of relieving the suffering of Gaza residents. Besides, the
people of Gaza do, in fact, have access to food, medicine, and
relief supplies—they are provided by both Egypt *and* Israel. The

flotilla was organized by the Turkish group Insani Yardim Vakfi (Humanitarian Relief Foundation), which Israel has placed on its terror watch list because of its reported links to global Jihadist terrorist movements, including Al Qaeda.[115] This fact should have been released before the commandos boarded the flotilla.

Why release a video days after the event, and with Hebrew subtitles? Why not show sooner that there wasn't much humanitarian aid on the flotilla but there were, in fact, many weapons on board? And why not show very clearly Israeli soldiers being attacked first? Ironically, one of the Israeli helicopters that was supposed to take pictures and transmit them to the media immediately instead had to transfer one of the terrorists to a hospital. It took a lot of time to get any footage so we were late in terms of PR. This very bad situation for Israel was made worse by the fact that those in charge of media relations did not do an effective job of controlling the narrative in the press or in the public square. With all due respect, our communications people must have known the ships were coming and should have had material prepared.

The flotilla event provided the government with a crash course on the power of social media. Images of the on-board conflict spread around the world like lightning via YouTube. Even now, after Israel got hammered in the foreign media, there is no wake-up call in sight, no explanation. Sometimes Israel believes its justified cause would uphold its image in the public eye. While that may be true in some cases, a justified cause is not enough to be right these days—in politics or in business. Anyway, being right does not help you frame the debate, nor does it keep you from being constantly on the defense. It's not enough to simple convey a message—you need people to see and listen to your position.

There are positive signs that Israel is moving more quickly to stop false news stories from taking hold in the public imagination.

We are getting better at fighting propaganda, especially the kind that can lead directly to incitement and violence. In March 2012, Israel acted quickly to quash a false and potentially extremely damaging tweet that went around the world very quickly. Khulood Badawi, an Arab Israeli information and media coordinator for OCHA, the United Nations' Office for the Coordination of Humanitarian Affairs, posted a link to the picture of a young girl covered in blood being carried by her father, along with the tweet: "Palestine is bleeding. Another child killed by #Israel . . . Another father carrying his child to a Grave in #Gaza." It became the top tweet of the day for anything related to Gaza. It is a common tactic of activists to produce highly provocative misinformation such as this.[116]

Except that that picture and story were false. In fact, the photograph was published in 2006 by the news agency Reuters along with a report that the girl had died in an accident at home, and most certainly not at the hands of the Israeli military. After I approached the Israeli minister for foreign affairs about the situation, ambassador to the U.N. Ron Prosor expressed outrage at Badawi's conduct and called for her dismissal shortly after the tweet and photo went viral. "We have before us an OCHA information officer who was directly engaged in spreading misinformation," Prosor wrote in a letter to the United Nations. Israel is also getting better at using social media to fight back. Foreign Ministry spokesman Yigal Palmor posted the following on his Facebook page: "Not only does a UN official in the Territories post a picture with a false description that demonizes Israel through a furious fabrication of facts, but her superior, Max Gaylard (Humanitarian Coordinator, mind you . . .) gives her full backing, and their New York HQ dismisses the outrage as a private opinion, unrelated to the UN. . . . The UN? Whatever."

As of March 2012, Badawi had not been fired, and offered a tepid response to her highly prejudicial misinformation via her Twitter account: "Correction: I tweeted the photo believing it was from the last round of violence & it turned out to be from 2006. This is my personal account."[117] This is the kind of opposition activity we face every day—in this case we caught and corrected it, but unfortunately we have to deal with the fact that this falsehood, and others, will continue to be spread on the Internet. Still, because of our efforts to unmask the blatant and inflammatory lie, the story did get a great deal of press coverage in Israel and on the Internet—at least in this case the truth prevailed.

There is no denying the historic and religious ties that result from the United States and Israel's shared Judeo-Christian heritage. The United States is one of the most religious countries in the world, so it is obvious that the return of the Jewish people to their historic homeland after thousands of years in exile was an event of much significance to millions of Americans. Our shared values of democracy, liberalism, and human rights also have contributed to the Israeli-U.S. relationship. Even now, while the world hopes for positive results that may or may not follow the Arab Spring, Israel remains the only true democracy in the Middle East and North Africa, where the civil rights of all its citizens are respected and leaders answer directly to the people in regular, free, and open elections. The American people recognize and respect this important distinction.

The Obama administration claims that it is trying to help Israel by enacting a "balanced" approach to our conflict with the Palestinians. While this new policy may be the result of a genuine belief that "balance" can alter the reality that we have had to deal with in our region for almost 100 years, this is not how it is perceived by many in the region. It is clear that extremist elements are instead emboldened by the distance that has become apparent between the United States and Israel. While I respect Mr. Obama's attempts at solving the bloody conflict, I would advise him not to abandon the principle of "zero daylight" between the United States and Israel on the core issues we face. This special relationship is not an act of American charity. It is a strategic alliance that greatly benefits two like-minded countries that share a common heritage and values. I urge all presidents, current and future, to assess whether this can be said of any other country in the Middle East.

PART 2

HOW ISRAEL ARRIVED AT THE CROSSROAD

FOR OVER 60 YEARS, THE AMERICAN-ISRAELI RELATION-ship has been, by and large, a close one, mainly due to the affinity most American citizens have for Israel and its place in the Judeo-Christian tradition. Many have tried to explain and analyze America's support for Israel. I see this commitment as stemming from three important elements: complementary religious beliefs, shared values, and basic mutual strategic security needs. Certainly on an official level, the U.S.-Israeli relationship has been a constant—and some would say rare—point of bipartisanship throughout the decades. It was Democratic president Harry S. Truman who recognized the infant state before other nations established ties. Republican president Richard Nixon's nonstop airlift of needed weaponry during the 1973 Yom Kippur War ensured Israel's survival during that pivotal moment. Bill Clinton and George W. Bush are two more examples of presidents who agreed on very little domestically but continued to develop and expand the U.S. commitment to Israel's security and wellbeing.

Most of us, on both sides of the Atlantic, assumed that the election of President Barack Obama would assure the continuation of this long-standing friendship. Unfortunately, as I demonstrated in the previous section, American and Israeli supporters of this special relationship quickly began to notice a subtle but noticeable change in policy dynamics. This change points to a fundamental misunderstanding of the moral and strategic reasoning behind the relationship. More important, this shift in U.S. policy has not only laced Israel into a precarious position but also threatens to endanger American interests throughout the Middle East and the rest of the world.

This shift in policy perhaps serves to highlight the differences the two partners have had in the past. In fact, the support for Israel has wavered somewhat, with the ebbs and flows of political and strategic needs throughout the last 60 years. Taking another look at U.S.-Israeli history with a critical eye leads to the conclusion that Israel fares best when she makes decisions based on her own best interests, and not on the wants and needs of the U.S. government. Some of the material I will cite may well be familiar, yet reviewing key events as a whole demonstrates the absolute necessity of an Israel in charge of her own destiny. Certainly the United States and Israel should continue to be friends, and we should work to strengthen that friendship for the sake of both countries, but we also have to accept that what is politically expedient for one may not be so for the other.

THE ALLIES AND THE NAZIS, 1939–1944

The history of World War II is enormous, and my purpose is not to cover it here. Instead, I want to show how, even before Israel came into existence, there was a political and moral struggle when it came to the United States and the Jews. The very people in whom the Jews had the most faith—Americans—essentially abandoned the Jews in Europe during the Holocaust.

Racism was a problem in the United States in the 1930s and 1940s, especially against blacks and Jews. By 1939 anti-Semites had two primary motives: The first was keeping America out of the war raging across Europe, and the second was keeping as many European Jews out of America as possible. For the latter, there was widespread public support—which may have come not from specific or blatant anti-Semitism but from a general fear of foreigners of all stripes, part of a basic fear of the unknown. There were certainly no expectations among Jews and their supporters that well-known—and therefore influential—people would make appeals to stop the mass killings in Germany. Individuals such as Charles Lindbergh, for example, claimed publicly that Jews were trying, in part through ownership of the media, to draw America into the war. Henry Ford wrote relentlessly against "the Jewish plan to control the world" in his newspaper, the *Dearborn Independent.*

Perhaps the most stunning disappointment for Jews came from President Franklin D. Roosevelt. He swore he was a friend of the Jews. Moreover, part of the mythology of the president was that he was a champion of the "little guy," a humanitarian who held liberalism and tolerance in high regard. It was assumed this ideology reflected an inclination to help the Jews when they were trouble. But he essentially ignored the plight of Jews in Europe, despite the fact that he was aware early on of what was happening in Nazi-held territory, and furthermore, had opportunities to rescue Jews with minimal effort. He consciously chose not to.

Britain and the United States were well aware early on of the mass killings ("genocide" was not a term in wide use at the time). The Nazis certainly tried to conceal what they were doing, but activities on such a large scale were difficult to keep under wraps. Information on the Holocaust came first from neutral countries positioned near the border of Germany. "Neutral" Switzerland returned fleeing Jews to Nazi territory. Instead of helping or accepting refugees, the Swiss government actively aided the Nazis through gold transactions. In 1997 U.S. undersecretary of commerce Stuart Eizenstat released a 200-page report charging that Swiss purchases of Nazi-looted gold, including that seized from Holocaust victims, helped prolong the Third Reich's war effort.[1]

News of the emerging threats also came from Italy, which was of course part of the Axis. German soldiers and off-duty military police would talk of the death camps, so there was credible gossip that penetrated Axis lines to the Allies. Many U.S. diplomats were well aware of the unfolding tragedy—in 1941 the U.S. minister in Romania reported that Jews were being slaughtered and warned that Americans there were also in jeopardy.[2] Jews who managed to escape from death camps and couriers from the Polish underground also brought firsthand accounts to public attention. Journalists from around the world, stationed in various locales close to Axis territories, heard about the camps and reported on them. An avalanche of information accumulated and by 1941 the U.S. government finally publicly confirmed that the killings were going on. At a certain point, the FDR administration had to make a decision whether or not to rescue Jews from their fate when the opportunity arose.[3]

The key question of whether or not to act on behalf of European Jewry was treated by the administration as a policy question, not a moral one. For the State Department, which at the time was filled with many Arab sympathizers, the question was: What do you do with these refugees once they are rescued? Where would they go? At the time, the administration had a strict policy regarding who was eligible for U.S. citizenship. Without going into the history of U.S. immigration policy, it should be noted that the 1940s immigration policies had been in place since the 1920s[4] and were much more rigorous than they are today. Once the United States entered World War II, the State Department put stricter immigration policies into place out of concern that refugees could be easily blackmailed into working as German agents.[5] At any rate, having thousands of Jewish refugees pouring into the United States was not part of FDR's vision of America, and in large part the public stood behind him. In short, rescuing Jews would have caused political problems.

The British wanted to keep Jewish refugees out of Palestine, which was the most obvious choice for relocation in terms of both biblical and historical fact, international legal recognition (i.e., Balfour, San Remo Conference), and proximity. Roosevelt could have pressured the British to reconsider their position on Palestine and open it to immigration, but chose not to do so. That closed off two major avenues for rescuing the Jewish population of Europe.

Appeals from Jewish leaders and their supporters were met with a catchy slogan; "Rescue through victory" was the line used to appease those calling for action. In other words, the Jews could only be saved once Germany had been defeated. For the first few months of that claim, Jewish organizations fell into line, feeling they couldn't challenge the president's position. But as news of atrocities spread, there was turmoil within the Jewish community over the claim that safe rescue was impossible, and dissidents started publicly and loudly pressing for rescue. This created a set of political complications for Roosevelt's administration. Remember that America did not enter the war because it saw an urgent need to halt the mass killing of innocent people. It entered the war because Germany was sinking U.S. supply ships bringing military material and aid to Allied troops. The Japanese attack on the U.S. fleet at Pearl Harbor was the last straw. Liberating death camps was last on the list.

Auschwitz-Birkenau was particularly "efficient" at exterminations, and, in fact, the largest numbers of European Jews were killed there. In 1941 there was an experimental gassing of 850 malnourished and ill prisoners, and after that "success," mass murder became a daily routine at the camp. By mid-1942, mass gassing of Jews was conducted on an industrial-sized scale. Some estimates say as many as three million people eventually were murdered there either by gassing, shooting, or burning, or through starvation and disease.[6] The issue of bombing Auschwitz-Birkenau or railroads leading to that and other death camps was not a matter of public debate, so the president did not have to comment publicly.

There were numerous private requests made through the War Department asking that this bombing be done. Among those who called for bombing was a young Golda Meir, who went on to become the future prime minister of Israel. Researchers from the Wyman Institute for Holocaust Studies uncovered documents revealing that in 1944, Goldie Myerson (she changed her name in 1956) was one of a number of Jewish leaders who pleaded with the Roosevelt administration to bomb the camps, or at least transportation lines leading to them. Meir at the time was a senior official of the Histadrut, a Jewish labor federation in British Mandatory Palestine. She and her colleagues had received many harrowing messages from their Labor Zionist colleagues in Europe about Nazi atrocities. The authors of one such message described themselves as "separated from you by a sea of blood and continents heaped with corpses."[7]

The continued refusal to bomb stemmed from the same motive the administration used not to get involved in the war: What to do with refugees? The administration used a twisted logic to dissuade those who called for rescue actions: It would "take the burden or the curse off Hitler."[8] It's unknown whether or not Roosevelt ever considered bombing, as there is no documentation concerning it, or none that has been found to date. But such requests were consistently made to the War Department and we can assume that its inaction was in accord with the policy of the president. We know for a fact that the secretary of war, Henry L. Stimson, knew about the idea and rejected it out of hand.

The official position was that the administration would not expend resources on non-military objectives, such as rescuing Jews. The administration also didn't know how successful such an operation might be, although they must have known it was within their power to render the wholesale slaughter of Jews much more difficult. The common form letter reply from John McCloy, the U.S. assistant secretary of war, said such maneuvers were "impracticable" due to the fact that they would require the "diversion of considerable air support essential to the success of our forces now engaged in decisive operations." It was intimidating to get a reply saying that planes would have to be diverted, so typically there was no follow-up. But researchers have determined that the diversion excuse was just that—a fabrication.[9]

In fact, the War Department never examined the feasibility of bombing the camps. They simply did not want to do it as a matter of principle. Wartime records show that a multitude of U.S. and British aircraft were often flying over Auschwitz or within a few miles of it, but their targets were oil refineries. Diverting a plane less than five miles to the camps would have taken a matter of seconds. The Allies also ran numerous raids close to Auschwitz through late summer and early fall 1944, so there were untold opportunities to take strategic action at little cost. One of the pilots on those raids was future senator and presidential candidate George McGovern, who later expressed his life-long regret at being prevented from helping victims of the death camps.

As a child who grew up among Holocaust survivors who shared their harrowing stories in school on Holocaust Day, I have carried this frustration my entire life; the feeling that in our greatest hour of need the entire world abandoned us. Many Christians have told me they share my feelings of regret and sorrow, and it's a shock for many to learn that the "final solution" could have been prevented, or at least greatly minimized. This is a sad chapter in Jewish-American relations, but it is one everyone should be familiar with, especially Americans.

The other way Jews could have been saved from the Nazis would have been to simply allow them entry into the United States. This was quite feasible from a logistical point of view. Empty supply ships routinely came back to the United States after dropping off materials. These ships were often filled with concrete to provide enough ballast to ply the seas safely. Instead of concrete, they could have brought human cargo back.

The Jews could have also gone to Palestine, which had a large Jewish community that would have welcomed them, and was, in fact, already proclaimed a Jewish homeland at the Sam Remo Conference in 1920 by the international community, which I discuss at length in the next section. Unfortunately, in 1939 England closed its borders for fear of creating a firestorm of Arab reaction—reneging on many of the provisions of both Balfour in 1917 and the San Remo Conference of 1920.

Despite the claims of FDR's apologists[10] that there was little he could do beyond what was being done, there is a growing list of U.S. officials who now say otherwise. "We should have bombed it," President George W. Bush said on a visit to Israel's Yad Vashem Holocaust Memorial on January 11, 2008, after seeing an enlargement of an aerial reconnaissance photograph of Auschwitz that was taken in the spring of 1944. Similar statements have been made by President Bill Clinton; Cyrus Vance, when he was secretary of state in the Carter administration; U.S. senator and 1972 Democratic presidential nominee George McGovern; and U.S. senator Claiborne Pell, chairman of the Senate Foreign Relations Committee.

The immigration policies of the United States also kept many Jews from being saved. In the 1920s through the 1940s there was a quota system based on national origin, which was in turn based on fear of foreigners and communism. The American Congress referred to a census done in the 1890s, and if it was found, for example, that there were 100,000 people of Irish or Italian extraction registered as citizens, only a certain percentage of that number of Irish and Italian people could be admitted into the United States every year. Quota percentages varied from country to country, with the largest numbers open to people coming from Northern and Western Europe, and the smallest numbers coming from Eastern and Southern Europe. The basic idea was to keep Jews and Italian Catholics out of the United States. In general, Northern Europeans were perceived to be the most desirable.[11]

Roosevelt inherited this system, but he could have amended it and chose not to. Some historians argue that public sentiment favored such restricted immigration policies, and Roosevelt already had enough to deal with. However, he could have done and said nothing and *still* allowed 27,000 Jews to escape Germany before the killing started. The quota from Germany was about 27,000 each year. In the 1930s Germany was trying to get rid of Jews, and this was widely known. The Germans would have gladly let them leave the country, no questions asked. And America could have absorbed them without fanfare.

In fact, the number of German immigrants during the thirties and forties never came close to 27,000. During many years the numbers were closer to 2,000 or 3,000, so the quotas went largely unfilled. In fact, the full quota was filled in only one year out of twenty. Even at the point when the Americans knew Jews were being killed it would have been easy to let Jews leave Europe and come to America. But at the time, the most powerful anti-Semite in America was Breckinridge Long, an affluent Democrat from Missouri who was the U.S. State Department's supervisor of the Immigrant Visa Section, ironically the man charged with helping Europe's Jews. A former ambassador to Italy and an admirer of Mussolini, he complained of "Jewish agitators [who] all hate me."[12] He deliberately created bureaucratic obstacles for refugees seeking visas and even found ways to block many humanitarian efforts. As a result, 90 percent of the immigration quotas from countries controlled by Germany and Italy were never filled because of the onerous application process.

Roosevelt could have directed the State Department to fill the quotas, told Long to remove the obstacles, and that would have been it. From 1943 to 1945 there were 190,000 unused immigrations spots,[13] so without lifting a finger he could have saved that many souls by simply following procedures already in place. But FDR and the State Department shared a vision of the United States, part of which meant limiting the number of Jews in the population.

Of course, the Americans and Allies did eventually liberate the death camps and the Nazis were defeated, but not before six million Jews and many millions of others, including men and women who helped Jews, as well as homosexuals, gypsies, and others, were murdered. The Holocaust is the legacy of the Jews and it is a memory that burns within us—one that we can never forget and that does and must inform our defense going forward.

THE OFFICIAL CREATION OF THE JEWISH STATE IN 1948

The story of U.S. recognition of the new State of Israel is a complex one, full of twists and turns. But I think it is worth going over in some detail, especially since many of the initial issues and debates are ongoing. America's policies toward Israel were often confused and contradictory, as officials tried to sort out what was in the best interests of the United States. If Israel had had to depend on U.S. support through this difficult but exhilarating time, she might not have made it. As often happens, history is a much messier affair than conventional hindsight recalls.

The creation of Israel in 1948 came after more than 50 years of attempts to establish a sovereign state as a homeland for Jews. Theodor Herzl, founder of the Zionist movement, initiated these efforts in the 1890s. His work gained momentum after the Balfour Declaration of 1917, which outlined the British government's support for the creation of a Jewish homeland in Palestine. With the dissolution of the Ottoman Empire after World War I, England was mandated by the League of Nations to rule Palestine. As Jewish immigration steadily increased, so did violence between Palestine's Jewish and Arab communities. Britain tried to restrict immigration, but this move was countered by international support for the creation of a Jewish homeland, particularly following World War II. This support led to the 1947 U.N. partition plan, which divided Palestine into small autonomous Jewish and Arab states, with Jerusalem under U.N. administration. Jews everywhere were gathered around the radio waiting for the counting of the vote: 33 for and 14 against. Many feared that such a tiny state would be indefensible, but at last the Jews had their land back and they could finally call it their own.

On May 14, 1948, soon after the British left Palestine, the State of Israel was proclaimed. Almost simultaneously, invading armies were dispatched from neighboring Arab states that refused to accept the U.N. partition plan. This conflict, called Israel's War of Independence, ended in armistice agreements between Israel, Egypt, Jordan, Lebanon, and Syria in 1949, and resulted in a 50 percent increase in Israeli territory.

What is often forgotten in this history is America's initial reaction to the creation of Israel. President Harry Truman is generally seen as a supporter of Israel and lauded for his recognition of the state. But at the time this was hardly the case. There was much heated disagreement within the administration concerning the recognition of Israel, predominantly coming from those in the State Department who valued ties to the Arab world because of the oil it possessed. The question for many in the administration, and Truman as well, was: Is it more beneficial to be friends with tens of thousands of Jews or tens of millions of Arabs? In effect, even after the United States recognized Israel it was a largely symbolic act, followed up with minimal support. When Egyptian planes were bombing Tel Aviv, the United States maintained a strict arms embargo on Israel. Israel did not receive a single bullet from President Truman. The Israelis requested steel plating from the United States in order to cover public buses, yet the State Department refused, classifying it as military aid and not strictly defensive.[14] The embargo was that extreme and wide-ranging. Recognition certainly had value later on, but Israel was isolated and had to buy damaged equipment from France, Czechoslovakia, or whoever was willing to sell. At the same time, the Russians were arming the Arabs with their most modern equipment. Truman further forbade American Jews from enlisting in the Israeli army.[15]

Even leading up to the creation of the Jewish State, relations were strained between Zionists and the governments of the United States and Britain. In 1939, Britain actually backtracked on its Balfour Declaration, disavowing the creation of a Jewish state in Palestine. Three years earlier, guerrilla fighting had broken out between Arabs and the Jewish population, and in the opening years of World War II, England believed she was not in a position to quell violence so far from her shores. Unwilling and unable to give this budding crisis the attention it required, she tried to placate both sides but in the end favored Arab interests. England clamped down on Palestinian Jews attempting to defend themselves. By 1939 Jewish immigration into Palestine was forbidden. Jews felt betrayed and looked to the United States for support.

Roosevelt initially seemed sympathetic to the Jewish cause but his assurances to the Arabs that the United States wouldn't intervene without consulting both parties put that position up for grabs. Confusion and indecision seemed to mar U.S. policy toward the Middle East at this crucial time. Flash-forward to August 1945, when Loy Henderson, director of the State Department's Near East Agency, wrote to Secretary of State James Byrnes that the United States would lose its moral prestige in the Middle East if it supported Jewish aspirations in Palestine. Yet in the same month, a report of the Intergovernment Committee on Refugees, called the Harrison Report, was very critical of the treatment of refugees, particularly Jewish refugees, by Allied forces in Germany. After reading the report Truman wrote to the British prime

minister Clement Attlee, urging him to allow a reasonable number of Europe's Jews to emigrate to Palestine. Truman also criticized the British White Paper, forbidding Jewish immigration to
Palestine, saying it was a dishonorable repudiation by Britain of
her obligations. In October 1945, Senators Robert Wagner of New
York and Robert Taft of Ohio introduced a resolution expressing support for a Jewish state in Palestine. But at a press conference on November 29, 1945, Truman expressed opposition to the
Taft-Wagner resolution and instead wanted to wait until he could
consider the report of the Anglo-American Committee of Inquiry
coming from England.

The Anglo-American Committee of Inquiry submitted its report in April 1946. It actually recommended that Britain immediately authorize the admission of 100,000 Jews into Palestine. In
May, Truman wrote to Prime Minister Attlee, citing the report and
expressing the hope that Britain would lift the barriers to Jewish
immigration to Palestine. Yet in June 1946, a Joint Chiefs of Staff
memo to the State-War-Navy Coordinating Committee warned
that if the United States used its military to enable Russian Jews
to emigrate to Palestine, the Soviet Union might retaliate in the
Middle East, which it was seeking to dominate. According to the
Truman Library, "The State-War-Navy Coordinating Committee
warns that if the United States uses armed force to support the
implementation of the recommendations of the report of the
Anglo-American Committee of Inquiry, the Soviet Union might be
able to increase its power and influence in the Middle East, and
United States access to Middle East oil could be jeopardized."[16] It
was an argument that would be made again and again. In fact, the
counsel to the president, Clark Clifford, wrote to Truman to warn
about the Soviet Union, arguing that the Russians would privately
encourage the emigration of Jews from Europe into Palestine yet

would publicly denounce the move in order to inflame Arab passions throughout the region.

Despite this, on October 4, 1946, the eve of Yom Kippur, Truman issued a statement indicating U.S. support for the creation of a "viable Jewish state." A few weeks later, Loy Henderson, director of the State Department's Near East Agency, fanned an additional fear of Truman's, as Clifford had, by saying that immigration of Jewish communists into Palestine might actually increase Soviet influence in the region. Yet despite his advisors' warnings, Truman kept pushing. In late October, he wrote to King Saud of Saudi Arabia, stating his belief "that a national home for the Jewish people should be established in Palestine."[17]

In February 1947, the British government announced it would terminate its mandate for Palestine and referred the Palestine question to the United Nations. In May 1947, the U.N. General Assembly appointed an 11-nation Special Committee on Palestine to study the Palestine problem and report by September 1947. In August, it issued a report, which recommended unanimously that Great Britain terminate its mandate for Palestine. Seven of the member states voted in favor of partitioning Palestine into Jewish and Arab states. This outcome produced a fierce conflict of ideology within the White House itself.

Less than a year away from the May 14, 1948, declaration of independence of Israel, on September 17, 1947, Secretary of State George Marshall addressed the U.N., saying that the United States was reluctant to endorse the partition of Palestine. A few days later, Loy Henderson, director of the State Department's Near East Agency, wrote a memo to Secretary of State George Marshall arguing against U.S. advocacy of the U.N. proposal to partition Palestine. And on October 10, 1947, the Joint Chiefs of Staff also wrote a memo, called "The Problem of Palestine," stating that partitioning Palestine into Jewish and Arab states would allow the Soviet Union to replace the United States and Great Britain as the overarching power in the region, and would endanger United States access to Middle East oil.

To complicate matters further, Herschel Johnson, United States deputy representative on the United Nations Security Council, announced in the same month, October, that the United States did, in fact, support the partition plan. Days later, Truman wrote to Senator Claude Pepper, saying, "I received about 35,000 pieces of mail and propaganda from the Jews in this country while this was pending. I put it all in a pile and struck a match to it—I never looked at a single one of the letters because I felt the United Nations Committee [United Nations Special Committee on Palestine] was acting in a judicial capacity and should not be interfered with."[18] Where exactly did the United States stand on this critical issue?

Then in early November 1947, a subcommittee of the United Nations Special Committee on Palestine established a timetable for British withdrawal from Palestine. In mid-November, Chaim Weizmann, the future president of Israel, met with President Truman and argued that the Negev region had great importance to the future Jewish state. The Negev is an arid region of southern Israel. According to the Book of Genesis, chapter 20, Abraham lived in the Negev after being banished from Egypt. Later on, the Tribe of Judah and the Tribe of Shimon also inhabited the Negev.

On November 29, 1947, the U.N. General Assembly approved the partition plan for Palestine, which divided the area into three entities: a Jewish state, an Arab state, and an international zone around Jerusalem. At the beginning of December, Truman wrote to former secretary of the treasury Henry Morgenthau, Jr., encouraging him to tell his Jewish friends that restraint and caution were in order. "The vote in the U.N.," Truman wrote, "is only the beginning and the Jews must now display tolerance and consideration for the other people in Palestine with whom they will necessarily have to be neighbors."[19] He also wrote to Chaim Weizmann, stating that it was essential that moderation be exercised if a peaceful settlement was to be reached in the Middle East. Just days after that, Secretary of State George Marshall announced that the State Department would impose an embargo on all shipments of arms to the Middle East.

In February 1948, Eddie Jacobson, a Jewish American businessman and longtime friend of the president, sent a telegram to Truman, requesting that the president meet in person with Chaim Weizmann. Truman refused at first, but Jacobson wasn't easily deterred. In March, Jacobson came to the White House without an appointment—imagine trying to do that today—and pleaded with Truman. The president famously responded with, "You win, you baldheaded son-of-a-bitch. I will see him." At the meeting in March, Truman assured Weizmann that he wished to see justice done in Palestine without bloodshed, and that if a Jewish state were declared and the United Nations remained stalled in its attempt to establish a temporary trusteeship over Palestine, the United States would recognize the new state immediately. He also promised Weizmann he would support partition—only to learn the next day that the American ambassador to the United Nations had voted for U.N. trusteeship.

Truman was enraged, and wrote a private note on his calendar: "The State Dept. pulled the rug from under me today. The first I know about it is what I read in the newspapers! Isn't that hell? I'm now in the position of a liar and double-crosser. I've never felt so low in my life." He also wrote to his sister, Mary Jane Truman, that the "striped pants conspirators" in the State Department had "completely balled up the Palestine situation," but that "it may work out anyway in spite of them." To his brother, John Vivian, he wrote of the situation, "I think the proper thing to do, and the thing I have been doing, is to do what I think is right and let them all go to hell."[20]

In April, Jacobson again entered the White House to see the president, this time going completely unnoticed by the guards at the East Gate. Jacobson remembered Truman strongly reaffirming the promises he had made to Weizmann, and, he wrote, "he gave me permission to tell Dr. Weizmann so, which I did. It was at this meeting that I also discussed with the President the vital matter of recognizing the new state, and to this he agreed with a whole heart."[21]

On May 12, 1948, Truman met in the Oval Office with Secretary of State George Marshall, Undersecretary of State Robert Lovett, Counsel to the President Clark Clifford, and several others to discuss the Palestine situation. Clifford argued in favor of recognizing the new Jewish State in accordance with the U.N. resolution of November 29, 1947. Marshall opposed this and actually told Truman that if he were to recognize the Jewish State, then he (Marshall) would vote against Truman in the next election.

Marshall and his respected deputy, Robert Lovett, made the case for delaying recognition—and according to historians, by "delay" Lovett really meant "deny." This was the beginning of the usage of the "right timing" motive to delay or deny decisions regarding Israel. When you do not agree with a friend, you put off the discussion—it's a common tactic. And the administration has used it many times, even including the stalled decision to move the American Embassy to Jerusalem, today. At any rate, the next day Chaim Weizmann wrote a letter to Truman, saying, "I deeply hope that the United States, which under your leadership has done so much to find a just solution [to the Palestine situation], will promptly recognize the Provisional Government of the new Jewish state. The world, I think, would regard it as especially appropriate that the greatest living democracy should be the first to welcome the newest into the family of nations."[22]

Then on May 14, David Ben-Gurion, Israel's first prime minister, read Israel's "Declaration of Independence." The British Mandate for Palestine expired, and the State of Israel came into being. Minutes after, Truman made his position clear, as the United States recognized Israel. The White House issued a statement that read, "This Government has been informed that a Jewish state has been proclaimed in Palestine, and recognition has been requested by the provisional government thereof. The United States recognizes the provisional government as the de facto authority of the State of Israel." Secretary of State Marshall sent a State Department official to the United Nations to prevent the entire United States delegation from resigning. On May 15, Egypt, Syria, Jordan, Lebanon, and Iraq attacked Israel. On January 25, 1949, a permanent government took office in Israel, following popular elections. A few days later, on January 31, the United States recognized Israel on a de jure basis.

Clark Clifford told Richard Holbrooke, with whom he collaborated on his memoir, that politics was not at the root of his position—moral conviction was. "Noting sharp divisions within the American Jewish community—the substantial anti-Zionist faction among leading Jews included the publishers of both the *Washington Post* and the *New York Times*—Clifford had told Truman in his famous 1947 blueprint for Truman's presidential campaign that a continued commitment to liberal political and economic policies was the key to Jewish support."[23]

You can see the machinations behind the scenes, and clearly the record shows how many foreign policy advisors were against

U.S. support for the creation of the State of Israel. Ultimately, it would not have mattered in terms of the creation of Israel, but our safety would have been in danger had the United States not supported the declaration. As Holbrooke noted in an editorial in the *Washington Post* on the sixtieth anniversary of the declaration of independence, Israel was going to come into existence no matter who recognized it. However, without early American support, Israel's survival would have been made that much more difficult—and nonrecognition would have marked another abandonment by the United States, following closely after the one during World War II.[24]

THE SUEZ CANAL

Between February 24 and July 20, 1949, Israel signed armistice agreements with Egypt, Lebanon, Jordan, and Syria. Iraq refused. On December 11, 1948, the United Nations adopted a resolution calling on the parties to negotiate peace and created a Palestine Conciliation Commission (PCC), including the United States, France, and Turkey. All of the Arab delegations voted against it. After 1949, the Arabs insisted that Israel accept the borders in the 1947 partition resolution and repatriate the Palestinian refugees before they would negotiate an end to the war they had initiated. This was a novel approach that the Arabs would use after subsequent defeats: the doctrine of the limited-liability war, where an aggressor can reject a compromise settlement and gamble on war to win everything, knowing that even if he looses he can insist on reinstating the status quo.[25]

Egypt had been confrontational with Israel even after the armistice agreement was signed. The first show of aggression was with the closing of the Suez Canal to Israeli shipping. This was in direct opposition to the armistice agreement. On August 9, 1949, the U.N. Mixed Armistice Commission upheld Israel's complaint that Egypt was illegally blocking the canal. U.N. negotiator Ralph Bunche stated: "There should be free movement for legitimate shipping and no vestiges of the wartime blockade should be allowed to remain, as they are inconsistent with both the letter and the spirit of the armistice agreements." On September 1, 1951, the U.N. Security Council ordered Egypt to open the canal to Israeli shipping, but Egypt refused.

In 1955, Egyptian president Gamal Abdel Nasser was able to import arms from the Soviets, which he would use in his confrontation with the Israelis. Nasser nationalized the Suez Canal for Egypt on July 26, 1956. Several months later, he sent the *fedayeen*, terrorists who had been trained and armed by Egyptian Intelligence, to engage in hostile action on the border and infiltrate Israel in order to commit sabotage and murder. On October 14, Nasser made clear his intent when he said,

> I am not solely fighting against Israel itself. My task is to deliver the Arab world from destruction through Israel's intrigue, which has its roots abroad. Our hatred is very strong. There is no sense in talking about peace with Israel. There is not even the smallest place for negotiations.[26]

Less than two weeks later, on October 25, Egypt signed a tripartite agreement with Syria and Jordan placing Nasser in command of all three armies.

The continued blockade of the Suez Canal and the Gulf of Aqaba to Israeli shipping, combined with the increased *fedayeen* terror attacks, prompted Israel, with the backing of Britain and France, to attack Egypt on October 29, 1956. The aggression by the *fedayeen* violated the armistice agreement, which prohibited hostilities initiated by paramilitary forces. However, in a foreshadowing of many such proclamations in the future, it was *Israel* that the U.N. Security Council condemned for its counterattacks.

Britain and France went to war with Egypt over concerns about the Suez Canal, not over Israel. Nasser's nationalization of the canal came as a surprise to British and French stockholders who owned the Suez Canal Company (SCC). Although Nasser promised that the SCC would be compensated for any losses, Britain and France were deeply skeptical and, together with Israel, planned in secret a military strategy to reclaim the canal.

The U.S. reaction to the entire Suez Canal fiasco is telling. The day after the October 29 attack, the United States sponsored a U.N. Security Council resolution calling on Israel to immediately withdraw from the area. England and France both vetoed it. In fact, the next day both countries bombed Egyptian airfields near Suez. Obviously the U.S. administration was upset when it found out that Britain, France, and Israel had planned a clandestine attack on Egypt. However, it's worth noting that when Eisenhower first came into office the administration was not particularly interested in promoting actions or policies that would help Israel, and Israel was well aware of his dispassionate stance. The assumption, which was proven correct, was that Eisenhower would not support Israel forcefully in the canal situation. The American focus was on communism at the time, and the Arabists in the State Department were convinced that helping Israel would give the communists an opening in the Middle East. Their reasoning was that, since many of the immigrants to Israel were from Russia, these émigrés probably included a fair share of communists. So during Eisenhower's first term there was a general lack of interest in and commitment to coming to Israel's aid.

Both England and France eventually agreed to a cease-fire; England made the first move after the Soviets threatened to intervene with "every kind of modern destructive weapon" to stop the attacks. The French wanted to keep fighting until they held the canal but couldn't succeed in convincing Britain to stay the course. The Eisenhower administration supported the cessation of hostilities, but without any formalized peace agreement from Egypt. Although abandoned by the two allies, the Israelis felt they had accomplished their goal in about 100 hours of fighting—they now held the Gaza Strip and had advanced to Sharm al-Sheikh along the Red Sea. Again, the Eisenhower administration opposed this outcome. The United States actually joined the Soviet Union to pressure Israel to withdraw.

In October, Eisenhower wrote to Ben-Gurion, saying: "Despite the present, temporary interests that Israel has in common with France and Britain, you ought not to forget that the strength of Israel and her future are bound up with the United States."[27]

The prime minister of Israel assured Eisenhower in November that it would withdraw its forces if the United Nations agreed to administer the Suez Canal area, which is what happened. Subsequently, Israeli forces withdrew from much of the territory of Egypt. However, Israeli forces still remained at the mouth of the Gulf of Aqaba, about 100 miles from the nearest Israeli territory. Israeli forces were also in the Gaza Strip.

This situation caused the largest rift between Israel and the U.S. government to date. Prime Minister Ben-Gurion took the position that Israel would not evacuate military forces from the Gaza Strip unless Israel retained the civil administration, including police. Nor would it withdraw from the Straits of Tiran unless freedom of passage was certain.

On February 20, 1957, Eisenhower broadcast an address to the American people displaying his anger over Israel's failure to totally withdraw its troops from these disputed regions. He acknowledged that Israel had been provoked, but made clear that the United States did not support Israel's actions:

> When I talked to you last October, I pointed out that the United States fully realized that military action against Egypt resulted from grave and repeated provocations. But I said also that the use of military force to solve international disputes could not be reconciled with the principles and purposes of the United Nations. I added that our country could not believe that resort to force and war would for long serve the permanent interests of the attacking nations, which were Britain, France and Israel. So I pledged that the United States would seek through the United Nations to end the conflict. We would strive to bring about a recall of the forces of invasion, and then make a renewed and earnest effort through that Organization to secure justice, under international law, for all the parties concerned. . . . Egypt ignored the United Nations in exercising belligerent rights in relation to Israeli shipping in the Suez Canal and in the Gulf of Aqaba. However, such violations constitute no justification for the armed invasion of Egypt by Israel which the United Nations is now seeking to undo.[28]

Eisenhower also raised the possibility of calling for U.N. sanctions against Israel:

> But the United Nations faces immediately the problem of what to do next. If it does nothing, if it accepts the ignoring of its repeated resolutions calling for the withdrawal of invading forces, then it will have admitted failure. That failure would be a blow to the authority and influence of the United Nations in the world

and to the hopes which humanity placed in the United Nations
as the means of achieving peace with justice.[29]

Ben-Gurion was trying to get guarantees from the United
States that Israeli ships could go through the Straits of Tiran and
the Suez Canal. It came to a point when the United States stopped
economic support of Israel. There was also a threat to outlaw
American Jewish organizations that aided Israel. Finally, U.S.
pressure resulted in an Israeli withdrawal from the areas it conquered, without obtaining any concessions from the Egyptians,
not even opening the canal to Israeli ships. This is what helped to
sow the seeds of the 1967 Six-Day War. One reason Israel agreed
to withdraw from land it had successfully taken was Eisenhower's
assurances to Ben-Gurion that Israel would have freedom of
movement in the Suez Canal. The administration sponsored a
U.N. resolution creating the United Nations Emergency Force
(UNEF) on November 20, 1956, to supervise the territories previously held and vacated by the Israelis. This temporarily stopped
attacks from the *fedayeen;* however, the attacks soon resumed,
this time carried out by a group of loosely related terror groups
that eventually became known as the Palestine Liberation
Organization, or PLO.[30]

Other problems occurred after the 1956 War—and before the
1967 Six-Day War—that continued to strain U.S.-Israeli relations.
For instance, the king of Saudi Arabia told the United States that
Israel was interfering with pilgrims making the hajj to Mecca
through the Red Sea. This accusation was patently untrue and
Israel said so. The United States said, stop the interference anyway.[31] Furthermore, the king insisted the Red Sea was an Arab
lake and Israelis had no right to use it, so the State Department
obligingly demanded that Israel tie up its ships in the area. Israel

complied. Then the king said there should not be any ships from Israel in the Red Sea, and the United States again told Israel to take its ships out of the water. Finally, Israel raised a logical argument: We fought a war in 1956 over the freedom of international waters; the Red Sea is not an Arab lake, and now the United States is telling us we have no right to use it? If we remove our ships, it would make no difference to Saudi Arabia. In fact, doing so didn't do one thing for peace.

By 1957 through 1958, Eisenhower began to reverse his views on Israel, but until then close relations with the Jewish State were seen as counter-productive to U.S. interests. The United States was trying to build up a relationship with the Saudis and maintain Arab allies in the region, in the hopes of turning them away from Soviet influence. The administration was furious that the British, French, and Israelis had gone behind Eisenhower's back on the eve of a presidential election. It saw these three countries as undermining its efforts to strengthen the United Nations and international action.

But by 1957–1958, a number of things happened that changed Eisenhower's position on Israel. Upheavals occurred in Jordan and Lebanon and U.S. troops were called in. A number of riots, as well as an externally inspired coup attempt that was personally thwarted by King Hussein, forced the king to impose martial law in the spring of 1957.[32] This was closely followed by a succession of internal upheavals, culminating in the crisis of July 1958. Five months after the formation of the Arab Federation, a federal union between Jordan and Iraq, a bloody military coup in Iraq by pro-Nasserist officers and led by Colonel Abdel Karim Qassem crushed the Arab Federation and left Jordan isolated. Israel was the only country willing to let Jordan use airspace to bring aid.

The Saudis said no, they had no plans to be helpful in any way. The Saudi king was duplicitous while the United States was trying to marginalize Nasser after the war. The Saudis were telling the United States how afraid they were of Nasser but they were supporting him, so the Arabs were seen as unreliable. The one country the United States could rely on was Israel. By the end of Eisenhower's second term, the administration came full circle, realizing that the Arabs and Saudis had no interest in peace. In fact, they wanted Israel to disappear.

Israel also showed its first intelligence capability in 1956, signaling its potential usefulness to the United States as a strategic ally when it came to information gathering. On February 25, 1956, at a secret session of the 20th Congress of the Communist Party of the Soviet Union (CPSU), Nikita Khrushchev, party first secretary, presented a serious attack on the policies of his late predecessor, Joseph Stalin. Included in the speech was a condemnation of the crimes against humanity committed by Stalin's followers. This speech was not intended for anyone other than the Communist delegates from party branches across the Soviet bloc because it was a quiet but startling reversal of years of propaganda that held Stalin up as a wise, wonderful, peaceful, and humane leader. The American CIA wanted a copy of the speech to expose the truth about Stalin to the world. But the CPSU was so secret it was impossible for an agent to penetrate its walls. However, Israel was able to deliver the speech to the United States. It was most likely due to a young Jewish journalist working for a Polish news agency, Victor Grayevski, who met Lucia Brenovsky, a senior person at the Communist Party in Warsaw. The two became friends and on a visit to her office, Grayevski noticed a copy of the speech on her desk. He asked if he could borrow it, and she said yes. He made a copy of the speech and, after reading it, decided to give the copy to the Israeli Embassy in Warsaw. Grayevski's parents had emigrated to Israel and the reporter himself had become disillusioned with Stalin and his totalitarianism in the early 1950s. The embassy, in turn, sent the speech to Israel, and leaders there sensed that providing a copy to the United States would prove the value of Israeli intelligence. It did. The speech was circulated across Western media and proved deeply embarrassing for the Soviets.[33]

THE SIX-DAY WAR, 1967

The Arabs are really strange people: They lose wars and then expect to gain by it.[34]

—Golda Meir, prime minister of Israel, 1969–1974

As Egypt built up its military capabilities during the Yemen civil war, which started in 1962, the Israelis, worried about the potential threat, asked America for both weapons and diplomatic help. Up to this point, U.S. military aid to Israel had been insignificant, but in 1963 the Americans approved the transfer of Hawk surface-to-air missiles to Israel. The Kennedy administration also recommitted itself to Israel's security and recognized the need to maintain a regional balance of power. By 1965, under President Lyndon B. Johnson, the United States also cut its economic assistance to Egypt, partly due to the increased economic burden of the Vietnam War but also because the Egyptian government wasn't yielding any positive results and was leaning ever more toward the Soviets. Russia would greatly exploit the Arab-Israeli conflict to win influence in the region, while denouncing so-called American imperialism to further promote pro-Soviet Arab unity.

During the run-up to the Six-Day War, there were a series of increasingly provocative incidents. Prime Minister Levi Eshkol said in a May 12, 1967, speech, "In view of the fourteen incidents of sabotage and infiltration perpetrated in the past month alone, Israel may have no other choice but to adopt suitable countermeasures against the focal points of sabotage. Israel will continue to take action to prevent any and all attempts to perpetrate sabotage within her territory. There will be no immunity for any state which aids or abets such acts."[35] On May 14, Israel learned that Egyptian troops had been put on alert and had begun reinforcing units in the Sinai "in impressive proportions and with unusual openness, artillery-towing trucks filled with combat-equipped soldiers rolling through Cairo's streets in broad daylight."[36] Foreign journalists in the area placed the size of the unit at a full army division.

But the United States refused to support Israel's efforts to defend herself. At the time, America was bogged down in Vietnam and was facing tremendous domestic opposition to the war. Protests on the home front were turning violent and growing in size. The United States didn't have the stomach for involvement with another war on an entirely different front. Instead of sending aid or troops, it tried very hard to find diplomatic solutions to the problem. For example, it tried to establish an international maritime presence to challenge the Egyptian blockade on Israeli shipping in the Straits of Tiran. That campaign ultimately failed. Still, right before the war, Johnson warned: "Israel will not be alone unless it decides to go alone."[37] After the war began, the State Department announced: "Our position is neutral in thought, word and deed."[38]

Even though the United States continued to refuse military aid to Israel, its position against unilateral Israeli action softened in early June 1967. Moreover, the Arabs were falsely accusing the

United States of airlifting supplies to Israel, even though Johnson had imposed an arms embargo on the region. France, Israel's other main arms supplier, also embargoed arms to Israel. In contrast, the Soviets were supplying arms to the Arabs. At the same time, Kuwait, Algeria, Saudi Arabia, and Iraq were each contributing troops and arms to the Egyptian, Syrian, and Jordanian fronts.

Despite this, Israel achieved a swift and decisive victory. In fact, an initial strike by Israeli fighter planes effectively neutralized the Egyptian Air Force. A ground attack launched a few hours later moved deep into the Sinai. President Nasser of Egypt lied to King Hussein of Jordan and told him that Egypt was winning the war.[39] Because of that, King Hussein of Jordan made a strategic and tactical error in entering the war on Egypt's side, which led to the swift destruction of the Jordanian Air Force. The Egyptian president lied again to Hussein in a famous telephone call where he told the king that American and British aircraft had participated in the fighting, defended Israeli airspace, and helped destroy Arab air forces. Perhaps he believed the lie because he found it unfathomable that Israeli's small air force could take out his air capability in such short order.[40] Today, with technological advancements like Internet satellite systems, he would have known what was happening, but back then it was possible to lie.

After Hussein rejected a June 5 Israeli cease-fire offer, Israeli defense troops moved into Judea and Samaria. Once again Israel was able to take control of the Gaza Strip and the Sinai Peninsula from Egypt, and Judea and Samaria, and East Jerusalem from Jordan, and the Golan Heights from Syria. Finally, the Jewish people were reunited with their ancestral land and the holy historical sites, including the City of David, the Old City of Jerusalem, and the Tomb of the Patriarchs.

The Wailing Wall, or the Western Wall of the Second Temple, is highly symbolic for Jews and was also liberated on the third day of the war, June 7, 1967. After the war of 1948, the Arabs were in control of the Jewish Quarter in Jerusalem and Jews were banned from praying at the Wall. Israeli parachutists completed the mission to liberate the Wall. Moshe Amirav, one of the paratroopers, describes his first minutes at the Wall: "Slowly, slowly I began to approach the Wall in fear and trembling like a pious cantor going to the lectern to lead the prayers. I approached it as the messenger of my father and my grandfather, of my great-grandfather and of all the generations in all the exiles who had never merited seeing it—and so they had sent me to represent them."[41] Abraham Duvdevani, another paratrooper, recounted that "I looked to the right and stopped dead. There was the Wall in all its grandeur and glory! I had never seen it before, but it was an old friend, impossible to mistake. Then I thought that I should not be there because the Wall belongs in the world of dreams and legends and I am real."[42] There were houses in front of the Wall, making it hard to get to, so the surrounding area was immediately demolished and cleared; on the first day of Shavuot, a quarter of a million Jews swarmed to the place.

After the war was over, the United States focused on determining who started it—the Arab states or Israelis—they also did not want the Russians to exploit instability in the area. On the evening of June 19, 1967, Johnson had a revealing conversation with J. William Fulbright, an Arkansas senator who was chairman of the Senate Foreign Relations Committee:

President Johnson and J. William Fulbright,

10.57pm, 19 June 1967

PRESIDENT JOHNSON: I think his [Soviet premier Alexsey Kosygin's] information about America's conduct in the Arab world is as faulty and inaccurate as his intelligence is on Nasser's capabilities.

J. WILLIAM FULBRIGHT: I think he must have known that. What I
meant is, he misrepresented it!

PRESIDENT JOHNSON: Oh, yes. But he didn't know it.

He wouldn't buy their [the Arabs'] statement that our
planes participated in bombing the Arab world. He wouldn't
take that one. But he did buy this stuff that we were there
inciting them. And there's no man in the world that did as
much and got condemned as much, by everybody from
Eshkol [Levi Shkolnik served as the third prime minister of
Israel from 1963 until his death from a heart attack in 1969]
on down, as I did—

FULBRIGHT: Yeah.

PRESIDENT JOHNSON: —for not inciting them. I told them [the
Israelis], I said, "You will not need to go alone unless you do
go alone. And we will take our time, and we will find some
way to open the Straits [of Tiran].

"But if you get out here, and cut loose, and act irrespon-
sibly, why, you'll develop a lot of sentiment in this country—
anti-Semitism, and every other damn thing. We just think it
would be highly irresponsible."

And we got them to put it off. They held it off for a
week—told us they'd hold it off for another week! But then
when Nasser said he was going to wipe them out, and he
moved this stuff up there, and Russia passed on the message
that he [Eshkol] was going to attack Syria, why, they couldn't
hold it anymore, and they had to jump.[43]

Johnson, it turns out, was greatly sympathetic toward Israel.
In May 2008, the Lyndon Johnson Presidential Library released
about 13 hours of recorded conversations that took place between January and April 1968 between the president and various

associates and colleagues. In one call with his ambassador to the United Nations, Arthur Goldberg, the president expressed his understanding of Israel's plight and reaffirmed the support for Israel that characterized his presidency. His own political standing was then in decline and the Vietnam War was going badly. He related his own underdog status to Israel's: "They haven't got many friends in the world," the president said, and "they're in about the same shape I am. And the closer I got—I face adversity, the closer I get to them. . . . Because I got a bunch of Arabs after me—about a hundred million of 'em, and there's just two million of us. So I can understand them a little bit."

On June 25, 1967, shortly after the Six-Day War, Johnson confronted the Soviet premier, Aleksei Kosygin, in a summit meeting at Glassboro, New Jersey. Kosygin recalled a conversation Johnson had with President Eisenhower later that evening. Kosygin couldn't understand why the Americans would want to support the Jews—three million people when there are a hundred million Arabs. Johnson's reply to his Soviet counterpart was blunt: "I told him that numbers do not determine what was right. We tried to do what was right regardless of the numbers." Aside from giving Israel critical diplomatic support during the Six-Day War and in U.N. debates that followed it, Johnson also supplied Israel with three significant arms packages, first in 1965 followed by one in 1966 and one in 1968. His policies also formed the basis for a U.S.-Israeli strategic partnership that continued throughout several decades, although it is being somewhat eroded today.

THE WAR OF ATTRITION AND THE YOM KIPPUR WAR

The War of Attrition was fought between Israel and Egypt from 1967 to 1970. In September 1967, Arab states formulated what is called the Three No's Policy, which barred peace and negotiations with, and recognition of, Israel. Egyptian president Gamal Abdel Nasser believed that military action was the only action that would force Israel to withdrawal fully from Sinai. Hostilities soon resumed along the Suez Canal. There was small-scale fighting between the two states starting in 1967, but on March 8, 1969, Nasser proclaimed the official launch of the War of Attrition, which included large-scale shelling along the canal, aerial warfare, and commando raids.

Rimon 20 was the code name of a planned aerial battle pitting the Israeli Air Force against Soviet fighter pilots stationed in Egypt during the war. On July 30, 1970, five Soviet-flown MiG-21s were downed by Israeli F-4 Phantoms and Mirage IIIs. Kissinger was afraid this would produce the "Sarajevo Effect," where a local dispute leads to a superpower dispute.

Kissinger employed the "carrot and stick" policy with Israel. The United States wanted Israel to stop bombing inside Egypt, and the administration thought military supplies would be the carrot to get us to stop fighting. It worked. We stopped the fighting in exchange for 18 Phantom aircraft. But U.S. secretary of state Henry Kissinger asked for compensation for the aircraft, and a promise that we would not attack new, very high-tech Soviet air missiles placed deep inside Egypt. That promise cost us a lot during the Yom Kippur War. Because we allowed Soviet ground-to-air missiles to be stationed in Egypt, we had to face them later. More than 20 aircraft were hit during the war, and most of them were lost.[44] That is an example of conflict of interest. On one hand, the United States wanted to show it was capable of stopping Israeli attacks and to show Egypt the great influence it had over Israel. Ultimately the decisions we made went against Israeli interests and endangered Israeli security. It was a mistake.

The year 1973 shows the price of acting diplomatically and not practically, and exposes the deadly effects of too much U.S. interference. Instead of engaging in a preemptive attack against the Arab nations that were gearing up once again at the borders, Israeli leadership succumbed to U.S. pressure, ultimately losing thousands of young lives in a surprise attack by Egypt and Syria. We reversed the tide despite heavy casualties—and learned an important lesson in the folly of sitting on our hands in the face of looming danger.

In 1971, Egyptian president Anwar Sadat suggested the possibility of signing an agreement with Israel, provided Israel agree to Resolution 242, which, according to Sadat's interpretation, would return all the land that had been won in 1967. No progress toward peace was made, however, so the following year, Sadat said war was inevitable and he was prepared to sacrifice one million soldiers in the showdown with Israel. His threat did not materialize that year. Throughout 1972, and for much of 1973, Sadat threatened war unless the United States forced Israel to accept his interpretation of Resolution 242 (see Appendix C).

Sadat appealed to the Soviets to provide Egypt with more offensive weapons to cross the Suez Canal. At the time, the Soviet Union was more concerned with maintaining an appearance of detente with the United States than in getting involved in a war in the Middle East, so it turned Sadat down. This decision made Sadat angry, so in retaliation he immediately expelled about 20,000 Soviet advisors from Egypt. In an April 1973 interview, Sadat again warned he would renew the war, but few believed him.

Then, on October 6, 1973, Yom Kippur, the holiest day in the Jewish calendar, Egypt and Syria opened a coordinated surprise attack against Israel. Yom Kippur is a day spent fasting and praying to atone with God. Even people who are not Orthodox or who are secular the rest of the year go to synagogue. Everything is shut down in Israel: No cars are running, no televisions are turned on, and no stores are open. Armies and hospitals run on skeleton crews. Arab strategists knew this was a special day; in fact they counted on it as a tactical strategy. About 180 Israeli tanks faced an onslaught of 1,400 Syrian tanks on the Golan Heights. Along the Suez Canal, tens of thousands of Egyptians attacked 436 Israeli soldiers. Nine Arab states and four non–Middle Eastern nations actively aided the Egyptian-Syrian war effort.

Two days before the war, a spy we had in Egypt went to Europe and met with one of our top intelligence people and shared the information about the impending attack. The issue of whether or not to call the reserves in came up. The chief of command wanted to call the reserves; Prime Minister Golda Meir did not allow him to do so. Her reasoning was that doing so would send a signal to neighbors and the world that Israel was getting ready for war. Reserves come from the community and there is no way to call them in secret. The prime minister was also, frankly, afraid of Kissinger's reaction—the idea was that if Israel "fired the first shot," we would be seen as aggressors. Golda Meir was afraid that such a move would so anger the United States that President Richard Nixon would not support Israel during the war, nor its policies afterward. It was a risk she was not willing to take. Kissinger essentially told Israel to wait and let him deal with the situation diplomatically. There was also pressure from the U.S. State Department on the Israeli Embassy not to fire the first shot. Doing so would be a crucial mistake.

Had we not been so worried about what Kissinger and President Nixon thought, and called the reserves a day before Yom Kippur, there would have been troops at the border that could have protected citizens and defended Israel. Golda Meir's inaction proved to be a fatal mistake. In fact, we should have made a preemptive attack because we knew what was coming. Nine Arab states and four non–Middle Eastern nations of Libya, Sudan, Algeria, and Morocco actively aided the Egyptian-Syrian war effort. On the Golan Heights, just 180 Israeli tanks faced 1,400 Syrian tanks. Along the Suez Canal tens of thousands of Egyptian soldiers, backed by 2,000 tanks and 550 aircraft, attacked less than 500 Israeli defenders with only three tanks.[45] As a result, 2,222 Israelis were killed and 7,251 more were injured, and 102 Israeli jets were shot down.

Israel was thrown into a dangerous defensive position during the first two days of fighting. Following brutal defeats during the first two days of fighting, Defense Minister Moshe Dayan was so disheartened by what he saw that he was close to announcing "the downfall of the 'Third Temple'" at a news conference. Prime Minister Golda Meir stopped him from doing so, but the episode demonstrates how bad things looked for Israel at that moment. The country mobilized reserves as quickly as possible and eventually pushed back, carrying the war deep into Syria and Egypt. Israel urgently needed more tanks, planes, and ammunition, but the Nixon White House responded tepidly by saying that it would only study the request. Facing the worst battlefield losses in Israeli history, Golda Meir offered to leave her command post to fly to Washington and personally plead with President Nixon to resupply Israel.

Finally, the promise of an airlift to rearm Israelis came from the White House. The cooperation would change the course of the war and begin a process that would forever alter relations between Jerusalem and Washington. "The President has agreed—and let me repeat this formally—that all your aircraft and tank losses will be replaced," U.S. secretary of state Henry Kissinger told the Israelis on October 9, 1973.[46] The U.S. decision allowed Israel to send hundreds of additional tanks and planes into battle and stave off future losses.

Because of U.S. pressure, Israel was not able to pursue the fruits of war to her advantage. As Israeli troops moved south into the Sinai Peninsula, they completely surrounded the Egyptian Third Army east of the Suez Canal. Many historians note that the Third Army was on the brink of collapse and could have been overcome by the Israeli army—but because of intense pressure from the United States we were prevented from destroying it.[47] When Kissinger found out that Israel had encircled the Third Army, he saw it as an opportunity to show that first, Egypt was dependent on the United States to prevent Israel from destroying its trapped army. Second, he could show Egypt that the United States had the power over Israel to tell it what to do. Kissinger's hope was that the show of U.S. strength could end the Soviets' influence over Egypt. The United States went so far as to threaten to support a U.N. resolution to force the Israelis to pull back to their hard-won October 22 positions if they did not allow non-military supplies to reach the army. In a phone call, Kissinger told Israeli ambassador Simcha Dinitz that the destruction of the Egyptian Third Army "is an option that does not exist."[48] Israel did not double down on the Third Army and by capitulating to Kissinger's demand lost an opportunity to show—literally through photographs and moving images—that we could dominate even when taken by surprise. This would have made for a different—and more positive—result in the long run for Israel.

Despite Israel's win, the Yom Kippur War gave the Arabs a lot of energy based on the belief that they could attack successfully and with stealth in the future. Indeed, the Arabs celebrate October 6 as a day of victory. They rejoice the fact that they were able to take us by surprise, destroy lives, and bring down a great deal of the Israeli Air Force. They march in the streets of Cairo each year, treating October 6 like a national holiday. I can only wonder how many lives could have been saved had Prime Minister Meir massed troops for the surprise attack and told Kissinger, I put the safety of my people before your ideas. I am not sure Egypt would have started the war had it known Israel was putting forces in place beforehand.

As a result of the war, the United States quadrupled foreign aid to Israel and eventually replaced France as Israel's largest arms supplier. The doctrine of maintaining Israel's "qualitative edge" over its neighbors came into being in the war's aftermath. In fact, many believe that after the Yom Kippur War Israel's enemies realized that they could not defeat Israel on the battlefield and turned instead to diplomatic warfare in an effort to weaken Israel's international diplomatic position. Because of pressure from the Arab world, most African and third world countries broke diplomatic relations with Israel after the war.[49] In 1975, the Soviet–Arab–third world bloc at the United Nations succeeded in passing Resolution 3379, which officially equated Zionism with racism in an attempt to de-legitimize the right of the Jewish people to return to their ancestral homeland. The resolution was finally revoked in December 1991, 16 years later.

THE RAID ON IRAQ'S NUCLEAR REACTOR

The year 1981 throws into high relief conflicting attitudes between the Israeli and the U.S. governments on carrying out military raids. Despite an overwhelming consensus on the dangers a nuclear Iraq posed for both regional and international stability, there was strong U.S. opposition to Israel attacking Iraq's nuclear facilities in a preemptive strike. Nevertheless, Prime Minister

Menachem Begin made the decision to bomb Saddam Hussein's reactor only after failure on the diplomatic front, and only after consulting military and intelligence experts. This event is key in thinking about Iran today and Israel's ability to take defensive action when it deems necessary.

President George H. W. Bush lauded the attack ten years later. Begin's decision proved to be right and contributed to peace in the world. In June 1991, during a visit to Israel after the Gulf War, then Defense Secretary Richard Cheney gave Major General Ivry, then commander of the Israeli Air Force, a satellite photograph of the destroyed reactor. On the photograph, Cheney wrote, "For General David Ivri, with thanks and appreciation for the outstanding job he did on the Iraqi Nuclear Program in 1981, which made our job much easier in Desert Storm."[50] In fact, America and the coalition forces might have faced a nuclear-armed Iraq during the Persian Gulf War (1991) and again during the U.S. invasion of Iraq in 2003 had Israel not bombed the reactors.[51]

The attack is probably one of the most famous operations conducted with F-16 fighters, and it was known as Operation Opera. It took place on a Sunday, the day when French workers would be off duty. Iraq established its nuclear program in the 1960s but was unable to make significant progress on it until the late 1970s. During that time they tried to buy a plutonium production reactor from France, as well as a reprocessing reactor, all necessary for the mass production of nuclear weapons. France denied the requests but did agree to build a "research" reactor and "research" laboratories. With French support, Iraq began construction of a 40-megawatt light-water nuclear reactor at the Al Tuwaitha Nuclear Center.

Israel engaged in an intense diplomatic effort to try to stop French financing and support for the Iraqi project. The Israelis knew that time was short: If diplomatic efforts failed, they would have to launch a military strike before the reactor was loaded with nuclear material to avoid the danger of nuclear fallout from an attack.

Israeli diplomacy engaged France; Italy, which was the main supplier to the reactor; and the United States. A high-level Israeli negotiating team, led by then Minister of Foreign Affairs Yitzchak Shamir, negotiated with French presidents Valery Giscard-D'Estaing and his successor, François Mitterrand. The French weren't interested in helping Israel, as Iraq was their top customer for military hardware. Payments came mostly in the form of oil, which the French needed and wanted. The Italians, also a major customer for Iraqi oil, were as uncooperative as the French. At this point any hope that the nuclear threat to Israel could be contained by diplomatic means rested solely on American cooperation.

In meetings with Defense Secretary Caspar Weinberger and Secretary of State Alexander Haig, there was agreement about the Israeli assessment regarding the Iraqi nuclear threat. American representatives even verified Israeli assessments that Iraq was working to reach nuclear capability and would exploit the ability to influence or destroy Israel. Despite the American consensus, America refused to act, perhaps because it did not truly grasp the danger, or, more realistically, because it did not want to upset Iraq, which was at that point fighting America's enemy, Iran.

Despite the failure of diplomacy, the Israeli government still engaged in a debate over the advisability of military action against the reactor. According to Yitzchak Shamir, some "greatly exaggerated the backlash that Israel would face." Prime Minister Begin decided to go ahead with the attack, but on the appointed day he received a note from his political rival Shimon Peres, saying, in effect, do not proceed because Peres opposed the operation on ideological grounds. Receiving such a note from someone who was not in the government at the time gave Prime Minister Begin pause. Was there a leak somewhere in his cabinet or elsewhere in the government? Did the media know? The Iraqis? He postponed the mission because of these worries, but eventually it was successfully carried out.

Shimon Peres, chairman of the Labor Alignment in the Knesset, tried to deter the government from carrying out the attack, claiming that Israel would be like a "thistle in the wilderness" after the operation. Other opinion makers and politicians on the left argued that the attack would unite the Arab world, could be considered an act of war, and would harm the peace agreement with Egypt. Some said it could lead to the counter destruction of Israel's nuclear reactor in Dimona, encourage an arms buildup in the Arab world, and lead to a European and American embargo on Israel.

According to Moshe Nissim, a former Israeli politician and a practicing lawyer, Begin became convinced of the urgency and necessity of destroying the reactor when he considered the danger of an atom bomb in the hands of a dangerous and irresponsible Arab ruler who would not hesitate to use it against Israel. In addition, Begin knew the Likud had a chance of losing the upcoming elections. If Shimon Peres came to power, Begin feared the plans to prevent Iraq from obtaining a nuclear arsenal would be shelved. According to Rafael Eitan, chief of staff at the time of the attack, Begin insisted that he "will not be the man in whose time there will be a second Holocaust."

Before the decision was made, Israel investigated a variety of options for destroying the reactor—commandos, paratroopers, helicopters, and Phantom jets. Israel also was not sure what Iraq's aerial defenses were capable of. The distance between Israel and Iraq was also a challenge—to fly over enemy territory undetected without refueling posed numerous difficulties. By 1979 Israel had discovered that recently acquired F-16s were capable of carrying two one-ton bombs at low altitude without refueling (although the plane did end up refueling).

From Lieutenant Colonel's Ze'ev Raz's (leader of the attack) briefing on the attack:

THE ROUTE: "We are about to fly a course over Eilat and Aquaba, and then south of Jordan along Saudi-Arabia's border. This route is planned to avoid Arab villages and cities where we might be discovered, so we will fly over desert area until Baghdad. This is not the shortest path to fly, but it would avoid radar detection, so we will remain undetected just until we get over target. On the way to the target we will fly at an altitude of 150 ft. On our way back we will fly at high altitude. We are short on fuel! Those who get engaged in dogfights won't make it back!"

THE BOMBING TECHNIQUE: "About 20 km east to the reactor we will ignite the afterburner to full power and start a climb. At the peak we will roll over, identify the target and dive at the speed of 600 knots at 35 degrees. Release the bombs at an altitude of 3,500 feet, aiming at the base of the structure, and release flares to avoid hits by ground fire. All pilots will drop their bombs in intervals of 5 seconds—You will drop 16 bombs in total, but a hit of 8 bombs could do the job!"

THE WEAPONS: "You will be armed with two 1,000 kg 'iron' bombs, equipped with delay fuses, to ensure explosion deep in the reactor's core to maximize the damage."

TARGET DEFENSE: "The reactor has its own air defense system, combined of AAA guns and missiles. Target is surrounded by high earth ramparts."

Colonel Ilan Ramon, who was killed on the space shuttle *Columbia* in 2003 and was number four of the first formation, describes the flight:

> We fly deep within Iraq. It is all desert around us while we pass another marking point on our route. I try to concentrate on flying my F-16, but from time to time I think about the target we are about to attack, and the responsibility we've got. It's the first time in my life that I really feel responsible for the destiny of a whole nation. The view changes—a blue river in the middle of the desert. We have been here 2500 years ago. . . . I see buildings and a deserted airfield. Somebody calls over the radio: "Watch out for AAA fire!" and the sky gets filled with flashes of exploding rounds. I light the afterburner and pull up. Just in front of my eyes I see the earth ramparts and behind it—you can't miss—the silver dome of the reactor. . . .
>
> "Eshkol 8" sounds the radio, "Everybody Charlie!" [Charlie was the code meaning all pilots have dropped their bombs.]
>
> It was amazing—I managed to see how the bombs of the pilots in front of me hit the target and the dome collapsed into the structure! The hits were excellent, and now we fly at high altitude back to our base. I hope they didn't start a chase, to run us out of fuel. . . .
>
> We cross the Arava and we are back in Israel. The IAF commander calls on the radio, and says: "All you have to do now is land."[52]

At the time, the attack was universally criticized. U.S. defense secretary Caspar Weinberger was stunned by the strike, according to secret British files released in December 2011. Sir Nicholas Henderson, Britain's ambassador to Washington, was with

Weinberger when news of the attack reached the defense secretary. "Weinberger says that he thinks Begin must have taken leave
of his senses. He is much disturbed by the Israeli reaction and possible consequences," Henderson cabled London.[53]

The United States voted for a U.N. Security Council resolution
condemning Israel and, as a punishment, delayed a shipment of
aircraft to Israel that had already been authorized. Resolution 487
said, among other things:

Deeply concerned about the danger to international peace and
security created by the premeditated Israeli air attack on Iraqi
nuclear installations on 7 June 1981, which could at any time ex-
plode the situation in the area, with grave consequences for the
vital interests of all States,

Considering that, under the terms of Article 2, paragraph 4,
of the Charter of the United Nations: "All Members shall refrain
in their international relations from the threat or use of force
against the territorial integrity or political independence of any
State, or in any other manner inconsistent with the purposes of
the United Nations,"

1. *Strongly condemns* the military attack by Israel in clear
violation of the Charter of the United Nations and the norms of
international conduct;

2. *Calls upon* Israel to refrain in the future from any such
acts or threats thereof;

3. *Further considers* that the said attack constitutes a serious
threat to the entire IAEA safeguards regime which is the foundation of the non-proliferation Treaty;

4. *Fully recognizes* the inalienable sovereign right of Iraq,
and all other States, especially the developing countries, to establish programmes of technological and nuclear development

to develop their economy and industry for peaceful purposes in accordance with their present and future needs and consistent with the internationally accepted objectives of preventing nuclear-weapons proliferation;

5. *Calls upon* Israel urgently to place its nuclear facilities under IAEA safeguards;

6. *Considers* that Iraq is entitled to appropriate redress for the destruction it has suffered, responsibility for which has been acknowledged by Israel;

7. *Requests* the Secretary-General to keep the Security Council regularly informed of the implementation of this resolution.[54]

The Israeli government explained its reasons for the attack in a statement, saying: "The atomic bombs which that reactor was capable of producing whether from enriched uranium or from plutonium, would be of the Hiroshima size. Thus a mortal danger to the people of Israel progressively arose. We again call upon them to desist from this horrifying, inhuman deed. . . . Under no circumstances will we allow an enemy to develop weapons of mass destruction against our people." The attack boldly reinforced Israel's doctrine regarding nuclear weapons. In terms of what is happening in Iran today, if one needed to speculate what Israel should do if world apathy continues, we can turn to the words of Menachem Begin: "Israel would not tolerate any nuclear weapons in the region."[55]

Preemptive, preventive strikes are risky for many reasons. But if done strategically, they buy time and provide immediate and urgent benefits. They may not be greeted with enthusiasm or admiration from the international community. So be it. Israel must be willing to make decisions that are unpopular around the globe and be willing to be condemned in the short term for such decisions in order to secure the wellbeing of our people.

OSLO ACCORDS

In 1993, the PLO and certain Israeli officials who were part of the recently elected Yitzhak Rabin government secretly negotiated the Oslo Accords in the Norway capital. The Accords granted the Palestinians the right to self-government on the Gaza Strip and in the city of Jericho through the creation of the Palestinian Authority. It also was a promise to renounce terror and incitement on behalf of the Palestinians. Yasser Arafat was appointed head of the PA and a timetable for elections was laid out that saw Arafat elected president in January 1996. Prime Minister Rabin and Arafat had outlined the treaty but wanted a U.S. presidential seal of approval. President Clinton may have been uneasy about the fact that he was not consulted on the negotiations—but he was nevertheless happy to take center stage at its signing.[56]

The signed agreement, called "Declaration of Principles on Interim Self-Government Arrangements," was focused on Israeli withdrawal from the territories of Judea and Samaria and the Gaza Strip, in order to allow the establishment of a Palestinian Authority for self-government during an interim period until permanent arrangements would be established.

The process began in January 1993 in a meeting with two Israelis, Yair Hirschfeld and Ron Pundak, and Palestinian representatives headed by Ahmed Qurei, aka Abu Alaa. The contact between the groups was made through Norwegian mediators, who contacted Yossi Beilin, a former Knesset member who represented the Labor Party. Beilin was appointed deputy minister of foreign affairs, and he officially acknowledged these talks, while depicting them as unofficial. Minister of Foreign Affairs Shimon Peres was updated by Beilin after the first meeting took place in January, and Peres informed Prime Minister Yitzhak Rabin in early February.

From its early stages, both parties spoke of an Israeli withdrawal from Gaza and the transfer of economic responsibilities in Judea and Samaria to the Palestinians. An initial draft of the declaration was made up in February and March. In April, Abu Alaa informed Hirschfeld on the Palestinian consensus not to include the subject of Jerusalem in the interim agreement, but he did ask for an official recognition in the negotiations. Rabin and Peres agreed to continue holding the talks by a representation of government officials, headed by Director General of the Ministry of Foreign Affairs Uri Savir.

Yosel Singer, who served in the Military Advocate General Unit and was later appointed as legal advisor to the Ministry of Foreign Affairs, had joined the talks in June. Prime Minister Rabin gave Singer his consent to formulate a new draft of the declaration, which was given to the Palestinians that June. The Declaration of Principles was initialed the following day. On August 27, Peres and the foreign minister of Norway, Johan Holst, reported to President Bill Clinton regarding the progress of the talks. The Americans who knew of the talks were doubtful, so when they learned they had been initialed they were amazed at the seeming progress the two sides had managed to make.

The signing of the declaration had dramatic consequences for the policy of Israel toward the PLO. Israel acknowledged the PLO as the representative of the Palestinian people and announced its intent to begin negotiations, as part of a comprehensive peace process in the Middle East. Arafat, in the name of the PLO, acknowledged Israel's right for a safe and peaceful existence. Arafat committed himself to the peace process and to working toward a peaceful solution to the conflict; he agreed to abstain from the use of terror and violent acts; he acknowledged the U.N. Security Council Resolutions 242 and 338; and he guaranteed necessary changes in the Palestinian manifest in the Palestinian National Council—mainly concerning chapters contradicting the declaration of principles or disapproval of Israel's right to exist.

Even after Oslo, while most Israelis were duped into a feeling of euphoria, Arafat clung to the phased destruction of Israel. In declarations from 1993 onward, he repeated the same mantra.

In any event, the signing ceremony was choreographed a mere four days after the document was presented to President Clinton. According to historian (and later Israel's ambassador to the United States) Michael Oren, President Clinton's role was not exactly as managing statesman, but as diplomat, "ensuring that both leaders attended the event and that Arafat would not attempt to kiss the reticent prime minister's cheeks."[57] The sight of historic enemies shaking hands on the White House lawn in September 1993 lifted spirits around the world. It raised great hopes that the Israeli-Palestinian conflict, one of the most intractable conflicts of the twentieth century, was on the verge of resolution. One of Oslo's architects, Yossi Beilin, argued that it demonstrated that no conflict, be it in Northern Ireland or in Kashmir, was truly insoluble. Both Arafat and Prime Minister Rabin went on to receive Nobel Peace Prizes, along with Simon Peres.

Unfortunately, the hastily signed U.S.-facilitated Oslo Accords resulted in anger from many Israelis and a deterioration of Israeli security as Israel suffered a deadly wave of terrorist attacks shortly thereafter. First, while many Israelis were hopeful the Accords would be the beginning of a real peace process, many others saw the idea that Israel would have to sacrifice Gaza and Judea and Samaria as a deadly move in terms of Israeli defense and security.

Large rallies and demonstrations were staged denouncing the government as surrendering Israeli security and statehood. Arafat was impotent to or was disinclined to rein in terrorist activities after the signing. For instance, an August 1995 bus bombing in Jerusalem engaged the passions of Israelis who saw the Accords as meaningless paperwork. On November 4, 1995, Yigal Amir, a radical far-right extremist who opposed the signing of the Oslo Accords, shot Prime Minister Rabin in the back after attending a peace rally. Rabin died, a sad moment in Israeli history.

President Bill Clinton donned the mediator's mantle in 1993 after Israel and the Palestine Liberation Organization signed the Oslo Accords. In negotiations between Israel and the new Palestinian Authority over the next step of the accords, Clinton clashed bitterly with Prime Minister Netanyahu, then in his first term as prime minister. The president persevered against pro-Israel critics in Congress and won agreement for a partial Israeli withdrawal from the West Bank.

Even today, we see the provisions of this accord disregarded by the Palestinians and their supporters—and if they continue to be broken, Israel will be obliged to ignore its decrees as well. Since the collapse of the Oslo process in 2000, a debate has raged as to what went wrong. Much of this debate has been a "blame game" designed to determine whether Israel or the Palestinians were more culpable for the collapse of the process. Of course, the PLO has reneged on the Oslo Accords again and again. The PA has failed to halt incitement and the teaching of hatred in schools, nor has it dismantled the organization's terrorist infrastructure. The PLO also has not changed its charter denying the existence of Israel. As recently as November 2011, the Palestinian attempt to declare statehood showed an utter disregard for the agreement. "By boycotting negotiations and by going instead to the United Nations, they [Palestinians] have reneged on a central tenet of Oslo," Prime Minister Netanyahu said during closed-door discussions in his office in November 2011.[58]

For over a century there has been a pattern: Many Jews have sought peace and conciliation and they have been met with violence. Even when the Arabs openly state that their only aim is Israel's destruction, many people have closed their eyes and ears and hoped that this time, after so many others, the work for peace will be sincere. All Jewish people are desperate for peace to reign but there are different ideas for how to achieve it. Many are blinded by false panaceas and promises, mostly made by their own leadership, that a new day is dawning if Israel goes the extra mile. Over and over again, Israelis are exhorted to concede more and more while the Arabs are only asked to stop incitement and killing.

Albert Einstein, in his wisdom, once defined insanity as "doing the same thing over and over again and expecting different results." This is Israel and its peace processes. Every few years the Israeli leadership revives the same plan and shakes the same hands, with the same declarations . . . yet peace has never moved even one step closer.

PART 3

A ROAD MAP FOR JEWISH VICTORY

ISRAEL'S SUCCESS STRENGTHENS THE UNITED STATES AND the civilized world. Why would any informed person want to put that success in jeopardy by diminishing Israel's place in the world, threatening its existence, or making its survival untenable by forcing it to abide by dangerously small and indefensible borders? Ancient Israel tells us much about civilization itself. Modern Israel shows us what human beings can accomplish in terms of democracy, free speech, and innovation despite both lack of natural resources and the fact that the focus of so many of Israel's greatest minds and efforts have been diverted to basic security. Once there is a viable peace in our region, all mankind will benefit from the innovations from our world-class scientists, doctors, artists, and manufacturers. And peace is achievable, although it won't happen overnight, through a piece of paper or a contract signed on the White House lawn. It can happen when all concerned parties in the Middle East come to the table and work for a logical solution.

It's essential to put my road map for peace in context, so it's understood why it is a necessary, logical, and positive step to take. To that end, I have to begin with a discussion of the biblical, archeological/historical, and political or legal reasons that Israel has a right to exist. These topics make some people uncomfortable—for instance, God and the Bible are not always popular talking points at sophisticated cocktail parties. I can only imagine the turn such conversations would take at soirees in urban centers. This discomfort is one reason why it is so important to address biblical rights as a way of stressing the absolute validity of a Jewish state. Despite being a secular country, Judaism and faith underpin much of Israeli society. I also speak to the remaining obstacles that prevent us from achieving a viable and lasting peace: why we must renounce the land-for-peace concept and insist that all partners in peace, specifically Jordan and Egypt, not only recognize but pledge to protect Israel's right to exist.

ISRAEL'S RIGHT TO EXIST

Nobody does Israel any service by proclaiming its "right to exist." Israel's right to exist, like that of the United States, Saudi Arabia and 152 other states, is axiomatic and unreserved. Israel's legitimacy is not suspended in midair awaiting acknowledgement. . . . There is certainly no other state, big or small, young or old, that would consider mere recognition of its "right to exist" a favor, or a negotiable concession.[1]

—Abba Eban, 1915–2002, Israeli diplomat and politician

It's amazing that in the twenty-first century we still have conversations about Israel's right to exist, because in some circles it's a topic open for discussion. The idea that Israel is the historic homeland of the Jewish people, and that Jerusalem is its holy capital, has been under attack from a variety of people, including politicians, scientists, major media representatives, and revisionist historians—many with respectable reputations. The right to exist is not a random claim made on an arbitrary piece of land, its name and area plucked from a hat stuffed with alternatives. The land where Israel sits is beautiful in my eyes, but it has always been in a rather tough neighborhood with few natural resources, aside from a few small areas near the sea and limited fertile ground for agricultural activity. In bare real estate terms, I can think of other, better-suited places where one might set up a country to thrive off the land. But Israel's physical place in the world is not an accident. The Jewish people have maintained ties to Israel for more than 3,700 years.

The Jewish people base their claim to the Land of Israel on a few basic premises aside from the fact that the territory was captured in defensive wars: (1) God promised the land to the patriarch Abraham; (2) the international community granted political sovereignty of Palestine to the Jewish people; (3) the Jewish people settled and developed an area that was previously basically a sparsely populated malarial wasteland.

BIBLICAL AND HISTORICAL RIGHTS

Despite the fact that Israel is a secular society, and one that includes a vast array of opinions and ideas, from atheism to hedonism, modern Israel is rooted in its passion for history, tradition, and knowledge of and love for the land. This enthusiasm shows all the features of biblical nationhood—a tie to the past and to our ancestors who trod this land before us, either physically or spiritually.

Open the Bible to nearly any page and take a walk with it. Israel is mentioned or referenced as many as 3,000 times in both the New and Old Testaments. You will see that in every description of the place there is a connection of Jews to the land (see Appendix D). And of course, if you do not believe that the Jews are connected to Israel, then you also cannot believe in Christianity as a religion or an event steeped in verifiable history. Judaism and Christianity are inextricably linked; even their Bibles are linked. And of course, Jesus was a Jew.

If you are not a "believer," instead look at the Old Testament as a historical document. It is impossible not to see the evidence of Israel's existence as a home for Israelites, or Jews. In biblical times the land we now know as Israel was referred to as the "land of Canaan." Essential to even a basic understanding of the Hebrew Scriptures is recognition of the connection between a specific area of land and a specific people in covenant with God. In the Bible, God gave Abraham, the first patriarch of Israel, the land of Canaan, renamed "Israel" by God, as an everlasting possession. Both the Canaanites and the Philistines had disappeared and ceased to exist as distinct peoples at least by the time of the Babylonian Captivity of Judea (586 B.C.E.).

The patriarch Abraham was told by God to leave his native land and his father's house for a land that God would show him. God promised to make of him a great nation, to bless him, make his name great, bless those who blessed him, and curse those who cursed him (Genesis 12:1–3). In 1741 B.C.E., Abraham began his long journey from Haran to Canaan—a journey that would have a great impact on the history of the world and a profound effect on the development of mankind.

Upon entering The Land, God told Abraham that it would be for him and his descendants as a pledge: "Unto thy seed will I give this land" (Genesis 12:7). Note that the term "Palestine" is rarely used in the Old Testament. When it is used, it refers only to the southwestern coastal area of Israel occupied by the Philistines. It is a translation of the Hebrew word "Pelesheth." The term is never used in the Old Testament to refer to the whole land occupied by Israel.[2] Abraham's son Isaac and his son Jacob lived in The Land until famine forced Jacob and his twelve sons to Egypt. Under harsh bondage, the descendants of Jacob, who was now renamed Israel, became a multitude but never gave up their identity under even the hardest of circumstances. After 40 years, God told Moses to bring the people out of Egypt and return them to their land. During the 40 years it took to reach their destination, God gave the people of Israel the Torah and the Tabernacle, both with an eye on the upcoming conquest of The Land.

The successor to Moses, Joshua, was instructed to rid The Land of most of its "idolatrous inhabitants," and again place The Land of Israel in the hands of the people of Israel. Each of Israel's sons became a tribe, and each tribe was allotted a part of the Land of Israel. However, it was not until King David that The Land was unified under one monarchy and the capital was moved from Hebron to Jerusalem, thus fulfilling the divine mandate. King David's son was honored to build The Temple in Jerusalem, which was to become the centerpiece of Jewish sovereignty and was the envy of and inspiration for much of the known world.

In 586 B.C.E., the Kingdom of Judah, the last holdout in The Land, was conquered and its Temple was destroyed. Its people were taken off into exile in Babylon. However, even during these cataclysmic times the people of Israel did not forget their land. In what would become a mantra for the people throughout all dark times, they pledged to remember their homeland: "If I forget thee, O Jerusalem, let my right hand forget its cunning. If I do not remember thee, let my tongue cleave to the roof of my mouth; if I do not set Jerusalem above my highest joy" (Psalms 137:5–6).

A few decades later, the people returned to their land and rebuilt The Temple. However, in 70 C.E. the people were again exiled from their land and The Temple was once again destroyed by a foreign power. This time the Romans destroyed the Israelite sovereignty and attempted to destroy the people and their way of life, as they had succeeded in doing with many others. However, they could not destroy what became known as the Jewish People, even though, according to historian Josephus, hundreds of thousands had been massacred and just as many sold into slavery.

As was common with Roman custom, all shreds of previous sovereignty were to be expunged and the Land of Israel was renamed Palaestina and Jerusalem, Aelia Capitolina. Palaestina was specifically chosen to remind the Jews of their earlier sworn enemies, the Philistines. The Jews that were left regrouped in places like Yavneh and Tiberias to form the body of law and tradition that would keep Jews close to Israel even during exile. Through the darkest moment of Jewish history, Jews forged an unbreakable chain with their homeland.

For the next almost two thousand years, Jews everywhere kept an intimate relationship with their land. Three times daily in prayer and every time bread was broken, the Jews would remember their land and beseech God to return them to it. At every festival and lifecycle moment Jews would tinge their happiness with the sadness that they were still in exile. Every Jewish groom at the peak of his happiness at his joyous wedding would break a glass to symbolize the destruction of The Temple and then incant the famous words from psalm 137.

As to The Land itself, there was a constant unbroken Jewish community there where Jews around the world would send their children to study and the old would go to spend their final years. No other people who conquered the land had the same attachment to Israel. None made Israel a sovereign power and none returned Jerusalem to its former glory. In fact, during almost a millennium and a half of Muslim rule, not one Muslim ruler made Jerusalem his capital.

Islam arose in the seventh century A.D. and immediately became a conquering and colonizing power, with an empire stretching across much of Asia, Africa, and Europe. As I discussed before, according to Islam, the world was split into two distinct areas, Dar-al-Salam (the House of Islamic Peace) and Dar-al-Harb (the House of War). Dar-al-Salam was an area where a Muslim ruled, even if Muslims were the minority, and Dar-al-Harb was an area where an infidel ruled, which, according to Islam, should be conquered and made Dar-al-Salam. Once an area was Dar-al-Salam, it could never return to Dar-al-Harb. The Land of Israel held no special importance beyond this status, and neither Palestine nor Jerusalem are mentioned anywhere in the Quran.

The biblical King Solomon became a ruler in approximately 967 B.C.E. His kingdom extended from the Euphrates River in the north to Egypt in the south. Solomon's greatest achievement was the building of the Holy Temple, Beit ha-Mikdash, in Jerusalem. Most of what is known about Solomon comes from biblical sources Kings I and Chronicles II. Even after the First Temple was destroyed by Babylon and rebuilt (the Second Temple was destroyed by the Romans), and Jews were exiled from the area, Jewish life in Israel continued unabated. Historians know there were substantial communities in Jerusalem and Tiberias in the ninth century A.D.[3] By the eleventh century, Jewish communities had grown and flourished in Rafah, Gaza, Ashkelon, Jaffa, and Caesarea. Although Crusaders killed scores of Jews in the twelfth century, over the next two centuries Jews reestablished themselves via rabbis and pilgrims who immigrated to Jerusalem and Galilee. Over the next 300 years, rabbis created Jewish communities in Safed. By the early nineteenth century, before the modern Zionists came into being, more than 10,000 Jews lived throughout what is today Israel.

History or archeological discoveries reconfirm what is found in the Bible—and in fact every archeological find in Israel and Jerusalem points to the fact that Jews were living there in large, organized communities. Perhaps one of the most exciting recent discoveries is the City of David, by Israeli archeologist Dr. Eilat Mazar, world authority on Jerusalem's past. Mazar's excavation took place in the southern shadow of the Temple Mount: Lying undisturbed for over 3,000 years was a massive structure that she believes is King David's palace. Within the dirt and between the stones, she uncovered pottery shards dating to the eleventh century B.C.E., the time when David established his monarchy. The City of David was the ancient nucleus of Jerusalem, located below the mountain on which the Holy Temples stood. From this focal point, the rest of the city as we know it grew and developed over the course of history.

Mazar believes that the palace was used for Jewish monarchs until the destruction of the First Temple 450 years later. As proof of this she offers a small piece of clay found at the site called a *bulla*, a disc inscribed in ancient Hebrew script with the name of the sender as a "return address," used to seal papyrus scroll "mail." The *bulla* bears the name of Yehuchal Ben Shelemiah, who is mentioned in Chapters 37 and 38 of the Book of Jeremiah. Yehuchal was one of two emissaries dispatched by King Tzidkiyahu to Jeremiah, asking him to pray for the people during the siege of Jerusalem by Nebuchadnezzar, King of Babylon. The *bulla* found on the site of the palace indicates that the king, or at least his ministers, used the building until the destruction of Jerusalem soon afterward. "For me, finding the bulla was tremendous," Mazar told a reporter.

"Yehuchal was no longer just some name in a biblical account that I might not even have been sure was true. He was a real person. We now have his business card. The account is a real account. It is very rare to find such precise evidence for a narrative in the Bible."[4]

The City of David is an important archeological site where you will find connections of the Jews to Jerusalem at every turn. You will see Dr. Mazar's palace excavation, an impressive structure from the period of the Judean kings. The Royal Acropolis and remnants of remarkable homes from the biblical period are also available for viewing. Even the underground water system from the time of Abraham, including recent discoveries of the Canaanite fortress that guarded ancient Jerusalem's main water source, the Gihon Spring, are open for inspection. After visiting the site, it is indeed difficult to deny the true history of Jews and their strong ties to Israel, which is one reason why most Israelis, including myself, welcome visitors to experience our history firsthand. I have learned from the experience of giving foreign dignitaries tours through City of David sites that after a couple of hours you don't need to say anything about our rights. They are well understood.

POLITICAL AND LEGAL RIGHTS

The Jewish people's claim to Israel is older and stronger than any other people's in the history of the world. The biblical connection of the Jews to Israel was noted in the previous section. However, some factors relating to the biblical and post-biblical era are important to note. For instance, the first Kingdom of Israel, almost 3,000 years ago, fulfilled functions of a nation, millennia before the modern notion of a nation-state existed. The Bible itself must have been one of the first documents that clearly delineate the borders of a state. The notion of nationalism, the right to constitute an independent or autonomous political community based on a shared history and common destiny, was first coined in the Book of Books.

The claim to sovereignty in the Land of Israel was not a new claim, but merely the reassertion of an ancient claim, older than the Greeks, the Romans, and certainly the British or French. The claim was never forgotten and can be seen clearly in everything the Jew did in his exile for two millennia. This attachment to one land with distinct borders and geographical locations has been referred to as a historical anomaly.

Whenever the Jew felt he had roots somewhere, there were those who told him otherwise and moved him along, often with the refrain to "Go home." The Jew was always considered an outsider in lands where he did his best to fit in, sometimes even throwing off all traces of his Judaism. As was witnessed all through history and most notably during the Holocaust, even total assimilation did not spare the Jew of his "different" status.

The modern era has seen the creation of many new states based on shared history and mission. However, since the destruction of Jewish sovereignty in 70 C.E., no people have ever attempted to make the Land of Israel a sovereign independent nation or state. This area was only ever a province in a much larger empire and was, for most of its history, largely ignored.

The movements of national unification and the rise of the nation-state are partly credited to Napoleon Bonaparte. During the siege of Acre in 1799, Napoleon prepared a proclamation declaring a Jewish state in Palestine, though he did not issue it. The siege was lost to the British and the plan was never carried out.

After centuries of living in a diaspora, the 1894 Dreyfus Affair in France shocked Jews into realizing they would not be safe from arbitrary anti-Semitism unless they had sole authority over their own land. The story begins with an obscure captain in the French army, Alfred Dreyfus, who came from a French Jewish family. Dreyfus might never be known had he not become a scapegoat in a case of espionage in the French army. In 1894 papers were discovered in a wastebasket in the office of a German military envoy that seemed to indicate that a French military officer was providing secret information to the German government. Dreyfus came under suspicion, most likely because he was a Jew—anti-Semitism was rampant in the army—and also because he had access to the same kind of information that had been supplied to the German agent. Army authorities said that Dreyfus's handwriting was similar to the writing found on the papers. Dreyfus claimed innocence but was denied access to the evidence against him. A journalist by the name of Theodor Herzl was very moved by this situation and attended the trial. Dreyfus was found guilty of treason in a secret military court-martial, stripped of his rank, and shipped off to Devil's Island for life.

That would have been the end of it had it not been for Lieutenant George Picquart, ironically a self-proclaimed anti-Semite. Picquart's anti-Semitism was overshadowed by his outrage that the espionage continued after Dreyfus's conviction. Despite his dislike of Jews, Picquart uncovered evidence that Dreyfus had been "railroaded" and that the officer who had actually committed the crime, Major Walsin Esterhazy, was still engaged in leaking secret information. He brought the new evidence to the attention of the army but they ignored it and acquitted Esterhazy.

Again, that might have been the end of it, but the novelist Émile Zola published a story about the cover-up in a daily newspaper. In 1899 the army conducted a new court-martial, and again found Dreyfus guilty, this time sentencing him to ten years of detention, commenting that there were "extenuating circumstances." The weight of the evidence, along with Zola's efforts to turn the matter into a cause célèbre, finally forced the president of France to pardon Dreyfus in 1899. In 1906—12 years after the case had begun—he was finally exonerated and restored to his former military rank. The "Dreyfus Affair" was one of the events that inspired the Zionist movement, founded in the late nineteenth century by secular Jews, because it exemplified growing anti-Semitism all over Europe.

After World War I, the "international community"—the British with the Balfour Declaration, the Allied victors at the San Remo Conference, the League of Nations, and the U.S. Congress—all called for establishment of a Jewish national home in the Holy Land.

Israel is, of course, the only state formed in the last century to be recognized by both the League of Nations and the United Nations. The British Mandate for Palestine was provided for by the League of Nations, which reaffirmed the Balfour Declaration. The British Mandate for Palestine did not create a new right of the Jews to a national home, but *confirmed a pre-existing right.* The document that created the mandate, and was ratified by all major powers at that time, recognized "the historical connection of the Jewish people with Palestine." The land area the British received as a mandate covered all of present-day Israel, the West Bank, Gaza, and the Hashemite Kingdom of Jordan. However, the British owed the Hashemites land after they lost their claim over Arabia to the Saud clan. Transjordan (later to be known as Jordan) was cut from the original mandate to create a new state, which was against the express wishes of the mandate. For more than one thousand years, there has been no Jewish presence in Jordan, and it is the same today.

Although many famous rabbis and figures declared that Jews should physically return to the land of their forefathers, none had much success until the end of the nineteenth century. Theodor Herzl, drawing on a wealth of scholarship and tradition, called for a return of Jewish sovereignty in the Land of Israel. At first, Herzl had few followers, but soon this movement, which became known as Zionism, attracted adherents across the globe and, significantly, the world's major powers.

Chaim Weizmann, originally a Russian biochemist who moved to England in 1905, was also a key figure in the Zionist movement and a member of the General Zionist Council. During World War I, Germany had a monopoly on the production of acetone, which was an important ingredient for arms production. In fact, the British might have lost the war if Weizmann had not invented a fermentation process that allowed them to manufacture their own liquid acetone. Weizmann's fermentation process brought him to the attention of David Lloyd George, Britain's minister of ammunitions, and Arthur James Balfour, former British prime minister and lord of the admiralty. Because of these associations, Weizmann was able to play a leading role in the Balfour Declaration of November 2, 1917, in which Britain committed itself to the establishment of a Jewish home in Palestine. Eventually Weizmann became the first president of Israel. The Balfour Declaration was issued on November 2, 1917, in the form of a letter from Balfour to Lord Rothschild, president of the British Zionist Federation.

The Balfour Declaration (in its entirety):

Foreign Office
November 2nd, 1917
Dear Lord Rothschild,

I have much pleasure in conveying to you, on behalf of His Majesty's Government, the following declaration of sympathy with Jewish Zionist aspirations which has been submitted to, and approved by, the Cabinet.

"His Majesty's Government view with favour the establishment in Palestine of a national home for the Jewish people, and will use their best endeavours to facilitate the achievement of this object, it being clearly understood that nothing shall be done which may prejudice the civil and religious rights of existing non-Jewish communities in Palestine, or the rights and political status enjoyed by Jews in any other country."

I should be grateful if you would bring this declaration to the knowledge of the Zionist Federation.

Yours sincerely,

Arthur James Balfour

Balfour was British foreign policy. Three years later, after World War I was over, at the Italian resort town of San Remo, on April 25, 1920, after two days of intense discussions, prime ministers and high-ranking diplomats of the victorious Allied powers signed the San Remo Resolution. It marked the first time in 1,800 years that the geographical region known as Palestine acquired a legal identity. The boundaries of Palestine were not precisely defined during the San Remo Conference; however, the idea was to draw them as close as possible to the historical boundaries of the ancient Jewish kingdoms of Israel and Judah.

By referring specifically to the Balfour Declaration of November 1917 and by reproducing the wording of it literally, the San Remo Resolution entrenched the provisions of the Balfour Declaration in international law. Thus, the *reconstitution* of the Jewish National Home in Palestine received international recognition. The legal title to Palestine was officially transferred from the League of

Nations—when Turkey was dispossessed of its rights to the region at the Paris Peace Conference a year earlier—to the Jewish people, who became the national beneficiary under a mandate awarded to Britain, thereby designated as the trustee.

The story of San Remo is important. In 1917 the war was still on and France, England, and the United States were allies against Germany, Turkey, and Austria. Most of the war happened in Europe and in 1918 the European powers met in Paris to decide the European questions. But there was still war raging in the Middle East, so they set aside the question of what to do about the Middle East until later. At any rate, most of the people in the British and U.S. governments were Christian, and they felt a connection to Israel and to the Jewish people, much like Christian evangelicals do today. Evangelicals, who are "biblically faithful" or see the Bible as a true historical document, feel this closeness to Israel because they believe the Bible teaches that the Jews must possess their own country in the Holy Land.[5] The British and Americans felt it was important to reconstitute Israel as it was 2,000 years ago. Balfour had the support of British foreign policy and had been approved by France and the United States but it did not have an international imprimatur. Once the war was over in the Middle East the allies decided to solve the problem of the Ottoman Empire. They could not do it in Europe in 1917 because the European problem was so complex, so they scheduled a meeting in San Remo in April 1920 specifically to settle the former possessions of the Turkish Empire, of which Palestine was part.

The four principal Allied powers of World War I, represented by the prime ministers of Britain (David Lloyd George), France (Alexandre Millerand), and Italy (Francesco Nitti), and Japan's ambassador, K. Matsui, attended the meeting. Americans were observers at San Remo because they did not participate in the war against Turkey. Reporters from the *New York Times,* the *London Times,* the *Manchester Guardian,* and from the French and Arab press were there as well so it is fruitless to deny the reality and importance of this event.

The officials combined the Balfour Declaration and the newly adopted Covenant of the League of Nations so that the provisions of Balfour became part of international law. The British people had not only a popular desire, at the time, but an obligation to carry out Balfour. By joining it with the Covenant of the League of Nations it became international law. They did the same for Syria and Iraq, which were distributed as mandates. For instance, Mesopotamia became Iraq, other parts became Syria, and so forth. Interestingly, no one questions the existence of Syria and Iraq, yet so many question Israel's.

The supreme council adopted the resolution in which they incorporated Balfour as international law, which was a novelty at the time because anytime someone conquered a country they created a colony. This was an enlightened position for the time, to give lands self-determination. It was President Woodrow Wilson's idea in 1918, which led to the creation of the League of Nations governed by a covenant. One specific article, 22, stipulated mandates for a limited period of time for a developed country to train and organize the future country for its own independence once it is are ready to acquire it.

The San Remo Resolution aimed for the establishment in Palestine of a "Jewish national home." Although Lord Balfour, Prime Minister Lloyd George, and many others understood this phrase as ultimately meaning the creation of a Jewish state, many British leaders attempted to dispel this notion in the following years. The British opponents to a Jewish state argued that the Jewish population was a minority in Palestine; that the Arabs would never accept a Jewish state in their midst; and that it would run against British interests, given the alleged need to appease the Arabs and the Muslim world as a whole, especially after the rise of Nazism in Europe.

But Balfour and others persisted in the ultimate objective of a state, as long as the Jewish population became large enough to establish a majority in at least part of the country. After all, the natural outcome of every mandate was to establish the sovereignty of the beneficiary over the mandated territory. Unfortunately, British policy from the mid-1920s to the end of World War II aimed at limiting Jewish immigration, contrary to the provisions of the mandate, which they were obligated to uphold, while turning a blind eye to the massive, illegal Arab immigration, as reported even in the Peel Commission Report, a British Royal Commission of Inquiry that set out to propose changes to the British Mandate for Palestine after the outbreak of the 1936–1939 Arab revolt in Palestine.[6] This is what prompted a number of underground Jewish organizations, notably the Irgun Tsvai Leumi (National Military Organization) and the Lohamei Herut Israel (Israel freedom fighters), to fight the British for their biased policy while at the same time defending the Jewish population against the incessant Arab attacks.

That is why it took more than 25 years before the State of Israel was proclaimed, with a significant Jewish majority. It must also be said that in 1948, following the appeal of Arab leaders to the local Arabs in Palestine to flee the country "temporarily," the exodus of 725,000 Arabs from Palestine helped strengthen the Jewish majority.[7] These people, together with their descendants to the fourth generation, constitute today the 4 to 5 million "Palestinian refugees," who are still kept in "refugee camps" throughout the Middle East under the control of the United Nations Relief and Works Agency (UNRWA). UNRWA for Palestinian refugees was originally founded as a humanitarian agency but has subordinated its role as a service provider to a political agenda. The UNRWA mandate is based on the idea of "right of return"—a right that in fact does not exist within international law. It maintains an unfortunate and destructive policy of keeping refugees in temporary situations— limbo—until they can return to homes and villages in Israel left more than half a century ago. The majority of these villages no longer exist. UNRWA will not consider resettlement. The false hope the organization gives to refugees promotes anger and radicalism within their ranks—and it denies these people basic human rights.[8]

The transfer of title and the sovereignty of the Jewish people in Palestine remain binding in international law to this day. Similarly, equivalent national rights were conferred to the Arabs in both Syria and Lebanon and present-day Iraq under two other transitional mandates awarded to France and Britain, respectively. It should therefore be apparent that the legitimacy of the present Arab states of Syria, Lebanon, and Iraq derives from the same international law, which *reconstituted* the Jewish nation in Palestine.

Besides fulfilling the national aspirations of the Jewish people (Zionism), the San Remo Conference also marked the end of the longest colonization in history. Whereas European powers extended their colonization in Africa, Asia, and the Americas for a period not exceeding four hundred years, Palestine has been occupied and colonized by a succession of foreign powers for about 1,900 years (Romans, Byzantines, Sassanid Persians, Arabs, Crusaders, Mameluks, and Ottoman Turks). This early episode of liberation, which preceded the global decolonization process by more than 30 years, should be welcome by all progressive minds.

In 1921, the British illegally created an autonomous political division called the Emirate of Transjordan that encompassed the entire East Bank of the River Jordan, cutting off two-thirds of the mandate and giving it to the Arabs in total. But on July 24, 1922, the Balfour Declaration was accepted by the League of Nations. Unfortunately, as I described in Part 2, in 1939, Britain reneged on the Balfour Declaration by issuing the White Paper, which stated that creating a Jewish state was no longer a British policy. It prevented millions of European Jews from escaping Nazi-occupied Europe to Palestine. Of course, the United Nations partition resolution of 1947, Israel's admission into the United Nations in 1949, and the recognition of Israel by most other states and nations further strengthen the political and legal right of the State to exist.

For the next three decades Jews from all over the world began the long journey home and the ingathering of the exiles began. However, the local Arabs were not interested in seeing Jews return and many formed armed militias to terrorize Jewish communities and dissuade others from returning. Such was the hatred for the Jews in some sections of the Arab community that the Arab leader Haj-Amin al-Husseini was the first leader in the world to congratulate Hitler on his rise to power in Germany and seek membership in the Nazi party. The mufti had risen in influence after inspiring, in 1920, the first major pogrom in Palestine against the Jews. The words "Muhammad's religion was born with the sword" were heard as Jewish blood was shed. The 1921 Jaffa riots occurred a year later as more Jews were viciously murdered.

However, the most horrific pogrom was the Hebron Massacre on August 23, 1929, where Arabs literally tore apart Jews, disemboweling, raping, and even roasting some alive while braying crowds watched on. Ultimately, 67 Jews were murdered. At the time, approximately 800 Jews lived in Hebron peacefully with tens of thousands of Arab neighbors. The summer leading up to the massacre was marked by unrest encouraged by the mufti. Arabs began to spread false rumors in their communities that Jews were carrying out wholesale killings of Arabs. At the same time, waves of Jewish immigrants were arriving in the area, which heightened Jewish-Arab tensions.[9]

On that August Friday evening, Arab youths started throwing rocks at the yeshiva students who lived in the neighborhood. In the afternoon, Arab rioters killed yeshiva student Shmuel Rosenholtz. On Saturday morning, Arabs came to the Jewish neighborhood carrying clubs, knives, and axes. The Arab women and children threw stones while the men ransacked Jewish houses and destroyed property. And of course, they violently killed men, women, and children. When the massacre finally ended days later, surviving Jews were forced to leave Hebron and resettle in Jerusalem.

After World War II, during the Nuremberg Trials, Adolf Eichmann's deputy Dieter Wisliceny testified during his war crimes trial in 1946 that "The Mufti [al-Husseini] was one of the initiators of the systematic extermination of European Jewry and had been a collaborator and adviser of Eichmann and Himmler in the execution of this plan. . . . He was one of Eichmann's best friends and had constantly incited him to accelerate the extermination measures. I heard him say, accompanied by Eichmann, he had visited incognito the gas chambers of Auschwitz."[10] Some historians have cast doubt on al-Husseini's involvement in the "final solution" since it was already under way after al-Husseini's arrival on the scene. However, he was a virulent anti-Semite and a tool of the Germans, helping them by broadcasting pro-Axis, anti-British, and anti-Jewish propaganda via radio to the Arab world; inciting violence against Jews; and recruiting young men of Islamic faith for service in the German military, Waffen-SS.[11]

In 1947, the United Nations passed a motion to partition the British Mandate for Palestine into two distinct areas, a Jewish state and an Arab state. The Jews accepted the partition and declared the State of Israel on May 14, 1948; the Arabs readied for war. The Declaration of Independence for the State of Israel drew a line from biblical times to the present by declaring "the Land of Israel was the birthplace of the Jewish people. Here their spiritual, religious and political identity was shaped. Here they first attained to statehood, created cultural values of national and universal significance and gave to the world the eternal Book of Books."

That same day Arabs attacked the new Israeli state; subsequently, armies from seven Arab nations tried to wipe out the newly formed Jewish State. Amazingly, the Jews won the war and gained even greater boundaries than originally granted them by the U.N. partition plan. Arab nationalism, which had been created at the beginning of the twentieth century, coupled with religious fervor could not accept a non-Muslim state in the Middle East, especially one that handed such a stunning defeat to so many Arab armies.

On November 29, 1947, the General Assembly of the United Nations voted with a two-thirds majority to partition western Palestine into a Jewish and an Arab state. This partition plan had been accepted by the Jews but rejected by the Arabs. This partition plan became null and void as a result of the Arab non-acceptance and the war of aggression placed on the newly declared State of Israel in May 1948.

When the war ended in 1949, Israel's new borders were set by armistice agreements. The armistice lines separating Israel from Judea and Samaria, or the West Bank, became known as the Green Line. In reality the line does not denote an official border, as is explicitly stated in the armistice agreements, where the Arab side wanted the agreement to refer to these lines for "military considerations only." The agreement continued: "The Armistice

Demarcation Lines defined in articles V and VI of this Agreement are agreed upon by the Parties without prejudice to future territorial settlements or boundary lines or to claims of either Party relating thereto." Thus these lines were never considered official borders largely because the Arabs were not ready for set borders, which would have meant acceptance of Israel.

The area beyond the "Green Line" was thus occupied and annexed by Jordan; however, this annexation was only recognized by the United Kingdom.[12] Thus this area had no defining sovereignty and the last applicable internationally binding agreement about this area was still the British Mandate for Palestine, which aimed to facilitate a Jewish national home.

Within minutes of the Declaration of Independence of the State of Israel, proclaimed on May 14, 1948, the United States recognized the newly formed Jewish State. This was followed by the Soviet Union, Guatemala, Byelorussia, the Ukraine, Poland, Czechoslovakia, Uruguay, and Yugoslavia. After being turned down initially, in February 1949, Israel renewed its application for membership in the United Nations. On March 4, 1949, the Security Council recommended to the General Assembly that it be admitted. On May 11, Israel was admitted, to become the fifty-ninth member. This granted Israel full rights as a member of established sovereign nations.

In 1967, as a result of the Six-Day War, Israel reunited Jerusalem and liberated the Golan Heights, Sinai, the Gaza Strip, and Judea and Samaria in defensive actions. The West Bank is commonly referred to as "illegally occupied territories," though this term is far from being definitively correct. The term "occupation" in the legal sense is derived from the 1949 Fourth Geneva Convention. It should be noted at first that to create an occupation, contrary to many false assertions, is not by definition illegal as there is no

law against occupying a piece of land. There are laws against taking land in an aggressive war, which was clearly not the case, but
there is no law against occupying land won in a defensive war. The
Geneva Conventions do, however, create legal situations as to the
administration of "occupied territories."

The Geneva Conventions were ratified by established states,
which were referred to as "high contracting parties." This, of course,
includes Israel. The land that Israel captured in the West Bank was
not under any sovereignty by any "high contracting party" and
thus could not be said to fall under the Geneva Convention. One
nation can only "occupy" another sovereign nation's territory; this
is clearly not the case in reference to the West Bank or Gaza. Former
U.S. State Department legal advisor Stephen Schwebel, who later
headed the International Court of Justice in the Hague, wrote in
1970 regarding Israel's case for control of the West Bank, "Where
the prior holder of territory had seized that territory unlawfully, the
state which subsequently takes that territory in the lawful exercise
of self-defense has, against that prior holder, better title."[13]

It is important to note that even the United Nations, with its
many anti-Israel resolutions, has never once called on Israel to
leave Judea and Samaria or Gaza. The most often repeated U.N.
resolution is U.N. Security Council Resolution 242, which does
not make this call. In fact Israel is only expected to withdraw "from
territories" to "secure and recognized boundaries" and not from
"the territories" or "all the territories" captured in the Six-Day
War. Even those against the wording of the resolution nonetheless
agreed with this interpretation. Vasily Kuznetsov, the Soviet delegate to the United Nations, said after the adoption of Resolution
242: "[Regarding] phrases such as 'secure and recognized boundaries' . . . there is certainly much leeway for different interpreta-
tions which retain for Israel the right to establish new boundaries

and to withdraw its troops only as far as the lines which it judges convenient." This is in addition to the agreement of the original drafters of the resolution, Lord Caradon of the United Kingdom and Arthur Goldberg of the United States, to this interpretation.

Between 1949 and 1967 the armistice lines hardly gave Israel any defense against constant attacks, with Arab armies able to shoot down onto the heavily populated coastal plain at will. Even the ultra-dovish Israeli foreign minister Abba Eban referred to the armistice lines as "Auschwitz borders." It is clear that "secure borders" as stated in the U.N. resolution did not mean a return to those lines. In fact, as Israel has given up the entire Sinai Peninsula and the Gaza Strip, totaling the vast majority of land won in the 1967 war, Israel has completely complied with the spirit and meaning of the law as cited in the U.N. resolution.

In 1964—three years before Israel "occupied" Judea and Samaria, "the territory"—the Palestine Liberation Organization was formed, which created the blueprint for all Arab and Muslim terrorism and rejectionism around the world ever since. Interestingly enough, the PLO never mentioned statehood but sought the destruction of Israel through armed struggle. This was to be the basis for many later terrorists; their mission was to destroy rather than build and to hate the other rather than give hope to their own.

As nations around the world started to afford the PLO more legitimacy, the organization became more ruthless and had more of a global reach. Muslim extremists everywhere were beginning to take notice. Groups like Al Qaeda have grown up with tales of the PLO and witnessed their ability to achieve political success while wielding the weapon. This was brought to devastating realization with the attacks on the World Trade Center in 2001 and other atrocities. The Jewish return to Israel and the Muslim and Arab violence that met Jews there was just one chapter in a struggle that is the defining story of a generation. To gain an understanding of where we go from here, we have to understand the histories that molded our present.

In conclusion, we should understand that when people refer to a "right," this can only be a legal definition. A people's aspirations or desires should not be confused with "rights." The State of Israel has many legal "rights" to exist, perhaps more so than most nations on earth due to its history. Israel also has full "rights" over Judea and Samaria, and there are no contrary claims that have any basis in international law.

THE TWO-STATE MISTAKE

What America and the international community can do is to state frankly what everyone knows—a lasting peace will involve two states for two peoples: Israel as a Jewish state and the homeland for the Jewish people, and the state of Palestine as the homeland for the Palestinian people, each state enjoying self-determination, mutual recognition, and peace.[14]

—Barack Obama, Washington, May 19, 2011

The fact is this: Your dream of a homeland has come true but you returned home to find that it was not vacant. You discovered that your land is also their land, the homeland of two peoples. And the hard reality is that there is no choice but for you to divide this land into two states for two people.[15]

—President Bill Clinton, the Israel Policy Forum Gala dinner,
Waldorf-Astoria Hotel, New York, Sunday, January 7, 2001

With all due respect to Presidents Obama and Clinton, those are not the facts. My mother was born in Palestine and she is called a

Palestinian on her birth certificate, even though she is a Jew and an Israeli. The idea of a Palestinian people is a modern construct. I do not deny that Palestinians today feel a communal identity that is driven by a variety of influences, not the least of which is a vision clouded by years of the PLO and PA teaching incitement and hatred and victimhood.

Historically speaking, Palestinians had been part of south Syria and had never been a separate nation under the Ottoman Empire. After international support and proclamations, the State of Israel was created in a peaceful, legal process by the United Nations. It was not created out of Palestinian lands, but rather out of the Ottoman Empire. The Turks, who ruled it for 400 years, lost possession of this land when their empire dissolved after siding with Germany and being defeated in World War I. Furthermore, there was no "Palestinian" land at that time or ever because there were no people who claimed to be, or identified themselves as, Palestinian. There were Arabs who lived in the region of Palestine. As Mark Twain famously described the region in *Innocents Abroad*, after traveling to the Holy Land in 1867: "Of all the lands there are for dismal scenery, I think Palestine must be the prince. The hills are barren, they are dull of color, they are unpicturesque in shape. The valleys are unsightly deserts fringed with a feeble vegetation that has an expression about it of being sorrowful and despondent.... Every outline is harsh, every feature is distinct, there is no perspective—distance works no enchantment here. It is a hopeless, dreary, heart-broken land."[16] and "There is not a solitary village throughout its whole extent—not for thirty miles in either direction. There are two or three small clusters of Bedouin tents, but not a single permanent habitation. One may ride ten miles hereabouts and not see ten human beings."[17] Numerous other visitors to the area recorded the same thing, such as Reverend

Samuel Manning, who wrote of the Sharon Plain, "the exquisite fertility and beauty of which made it to the Hebrew mind a symbol of prosperity. But where were the inhabitants? This fertile plain, which might support an immense population, is almost a solitude. . . . Day by day we were to learn afresh the lesson now forced upon us, that the denunciations of ancient prophecy have been fulfilled to the very letter—the land is left void and desolate and without inhabitants."[18]

Post–World War I also saw the creation of Jordan, Syria, Lebanon, and Iraq out of the former Turkish Empire. You can thank Britain and France, as the leading regional forces after the war ended, for this. In fact, Jordan was created on about 80 percent of the Palestine Mandate, which was originally designated by the League of Nations as part of the Jewish homeland. But since then, Jews have been prohibited from owning property in Jordan. Jordan is home to the majority of people who identify themselves as Palestinians. More than 2.7 million live in Jordan, or about 70 percent of the population.[19] One and a half million live in Judea and Samaria ("the West Bank"). More than 963,000 live in Gaza, and just over a million Arab Israelis live in Israel. In smaller numbers, Palestinians live in Lebanon, Syria, Egypt, Iraq, Libya, and of course the United States and other countries around the world.[20] Clearly, there is no historical or population-related evidence that Israel is the prime and only location for a Palestinian state.

More important than any manufactured claim to a Palestinian state is the fact that such an entity would be a serious and ongoing threat for Israel. I would ask someone in any state in America how they would feel if Al Qaeda or Iran or North Korea wanted to set up shop on its borders. No one would want to see such an outcome, but Israelis living near the border of Gaza experience this every day. In 2005, when Prime Minister Ariel Sharon decided to evacuate all the Jews from Gaza, Hamas stepped in and used Gaza as a base to launch rockets on major cities in Israel. A Palestinian state would be no different, and most probably worse, since funding and other aid would likely be greatly increased from those countries bent on seeing Israel's destruction. A Palestinian state would also have an army or have access to one, since it's difficult to think of a demilitarized state that is not protected by another nation's military. Once a military structure was in place, it is not difficult to imagine it working toward acquiring weapons of mass destruction, which would most assuredly be used against Israeli targets. You see the thirst for more weapons happening in Gaza today, so why would this not be the same in the Palestinian state?

A Palestinian state would also be impossible to deal with as a terror state, without putting many innocent civilian lives, both Israeli and Arab, at stake. For example, proximity is a major issue at Ben-Gurion Airport. When planes come in from Europe or the United States they must make a U-turn, and when this is done the plane goes directly above Judea and Samaria. One can imagine what would happen if that area was a Palestinian state with no Israeli control over security. One terrorist with one missile could take down a jet full of passengers. Along with loss of life in the air and on the ground, what would that do to the tourism and business climate in Israel? Exactly what the missile intended to do: ruin it. Before we gave Gaza up, I asked Prime Minister Ariel Sharon what we should do if it becomes a base of terror—which it has. His reply was we would move in with tanks and clean it up. But you cannot do that when you have civilians mixed in with terrorists, a play that is common—and cowardly, I might add. It is very hard to maintain stability, and that would be the case in Judea and Samaria if it were part of a Palestinian state. It does not matter how strong the air force would be because we would be unable to use it. And if we did, what a heavy price we would pay in terms of casualties and condemnation.

The creation of the PLO state and the murderous campaign it waged against Israel for the next few decades further forced all of Israel to realize that the only way the Arab world could relate to Israel was with its destruction. Indeed, the PLO understands something about the West and Israel, and its techniques have now been copycatted by terrorist groups such as Al Qaeda. These groups witnessed Israel easily winning wars against conventional armies, and the Arab nations unable to achieve their aims through conventional wars. The PLO knew that Israel and the West have an Achilles heel and that is their love of life and how easy it is to terrorize millions of people through a series of small but bloody tasks.

It should be noted at this point that the PLO terrorist network was attacking Israel years before the 1967 war and the subsequent liberation of Judea, Samaria, and Gaza. Here, a brief list of some of the PLO-sponsored terror attacks between 1965 and 1967:

Jan 1, 1965—Palestinian terrorists attempted to bomb the
National Water Carrier. This was the first attack carried out
by the PLO's Fatah faction.

Jul 5, 1965—A Fatah terrorism cell planted explosives at Mitzpe
Massua, near Beit Guvrin; and on the railroad tracks to
Jerusalem near Kafr Battir.

Nov 7, 1965—A Fatah terrorist cell that infiltrated from Jordan
blew up a house in Moshav Givat Yeshayahu, south of Beit
Shemesh. The house was destroyed, but the inhabitants
were miraculously unhurt.

Apr 25, 1966—Explosions placed by terrorists wounded two
civilians and damaged three houses in Moshav Beit Yosef,
in the Beit Shean Valley.

Jul 14, 1966—Terrorists attacked a house in Kfar Yuval, in the
North.

Jul 19, 1966—Terrorists infiltrated into Moshav Margaliot on the
northern border and planted nine explosive charges.

Jan 14, 1967—Terrorists laid a landmine at a soccer game that
exploded, killing 1 and injuring 2.[21]

There were also several attacks post-1967. One of the worst, in
1970, involved a Swiss Air flight bound for Tel Aviv. It was bombed
in mid-flight by PFLP, a PLO member group, and 47 people were
killed. Only a few months later after murdering children on a bus
to school in Moshav Avivim, the PLO hijacked TWA, Pan-Am, and
BOAC airplanes. The Munich Massacre of 1972 brought the PLO
their largest publicity as the Israeli Olympic team to Germany was
massacred while the world watched on their television screens.
The PLO did not just target Israelis; in 1973 Palestinian terrorists took over the Saudi Arabian Embassy in Khartoum, and the
U.S. ambassador was riddled with bullets at point-blank range
after Yasser Arafat gave the direct order, according to a State
Department report.

In 1974, the PNC, the legislative body of the PLO, approved
the Ten-Point Program, or the Phased Plan, formulated by Fatah's
leaders, which calls for the establishment of a national authority "over every part of Palestinian territory that is liberated" with
the aim of "completing the liberation of all Palestinian territory."
Amazingly some saw this as a massive compromise on the part
of the Arabs. This was a clear plan to extract concessions from
Israel in the guise of negotiations until all of Israel had been

compromised away. Again it is clear that the PLO understood how Israel's desperation for peace could cloud a whole document of hate and violence for one word of possible compromise.

Even as Arafat and the PLO were declaring the absolute destruction of Israel and murdering people all over the world, Arafat was being recognized as a legitimate political leader. In the same years as the Ten-Point Program, Arafat became the first representative of a nongovernmental organization to address a plenary session of the U.N. General Assembly. Even from the U.N. plenum he called for violence against Israelis while the world leaders looked on approvingly.

Arafat and the PLO had succeeded in only a few years to become the most well-known and bloody terrorists in the world and at the same time speak in a body that is supposedly dedicated to achieving world peace. The Arabs knew that their way of blood and fire had achieved their aims: legitimacy and conciliation.

While continuing to circle the world in kidnappings, hostage takings, hijackings, and murder, the PLO was also creating the guise that it only wanted to live in peace. After the First Intifada broke out in 1987, the PLO was caught off guard in Tunis, but soon took control of the situation in Judea, Samaria, and Gaza. While the Israeli public became fearful and the international community reacted in righteous indignation to Israel's defensive policies, Arafat and his cohorts sat back and enjoyed the focus of attention.

After openly supporting Saddam Hussein against most of the world in Iraq's invasion of Kuwait in 1990, Arafat realized that the West and Israel would disregard every act he perpetrated as they looked for a "peace partner." Already in 1988, the United States had started having diplomatic talks with the PLO, which had at last achieved respectability.

In 1993, the PLO and certain Israeli officials secretly negotiated the Oslo Accords. The Accords granted the Palestinians the
right to self-government in the Gaza Strip and the city of Jericho
through the creation of the Palestinian Authority. Yasser Arafat
was appointed head of the PA and a timetable for elections was
laid out that saw Arafat elected president in January 1996. To
many this signaled a turning point toward peace, and they were
desperate to grasp it, regardless of the fine print and the bellicose stance of Arafat. Even after Oslo, while most Israelis were
duped into a feeling of euphoria, Arafat still clung to the phased
destruction of Israel. In declarations from 1993 onward, he repeated the same mantra: "The struggle will continue until all of
Palestine is liberated." Even other PLO officials were brazen in
their comments and declaration of the ultimate destruction of
Israel.

On September 1, 1993, Yasser Arafat reaffirmed that the Oslo
Accords are an intrinsic part of the PLO's 1974 phased plan for
Israel's destruction: "The agreement will be a basis for an independent Palestinian state in accordance with the Palestinian National
Council resolution issued in 1974. . . . The PNC resolution issued
in 1974 calls for the establishment of a national authority on any
part of Palestinian soil from which Israel withdraws or which is
liberated." Later, on May 29, 1994, Rashid Abu Shbak, a senior PA
security official, remarked: "The light which has shone over Gaza
and Jericho will also reach the Negev and the Galilee."

Of course we now know that the PLO was true to its word and
initiated the Second Intifada, which again brought massacres
to the streets of all the major Israeli cities. However, again most
Israelis wanted to believe that they should stretch their hand
to the Arabs in peace and all the violence and rejection would
just disappear. This has been shown time and time again to be

a false premise. Every time Israelis cheered the signing of a new peace accord, deal, or plan, they would be met with violence and destruction.

Israel must clearly understand that its destiny should not be left to the goodwill of other nations. The Jews have always acted as a barometer for evil. Throughout history the Jews have been the "canary in the coal mine" that shows true evil and hatred as it truly is. The Arab rejectionism is the latest in a long line of people, movements, and ideologies that have spread their destruction around the world, but have always begun with the Jews. Many people suppose that the Arabs hate the West because of Israel, when in fact it is the other way around. The Arabs hate Israel because it *represents* the West, a bastion of freedom and democracy in a sea of dictatorships, backwardness, and repression.

Israel's mission is to remain in its land and seek its own peace, not based on concessions and conciliation. If Israel were to lose, the Arab rejectionists would achieve a sizeable victory that would spur them on to their greatest battle against the West. This should be unthinkable for anyone who values freedom and democracy.

THE IMMEDIATE PHASE

In the short term, we do not present any major change efforts. At this early stage, it's really about successful conflict management— a necessity to achieving conflict resolution. Since the current conflict is based not only on territorial demands but on a cultural conflict, you cannot appease the Arab side by giving in to land demands. Only after Israel shows strength and the ability to manage the conflict can we gradually move on to longer-term solutions. Part of this management does have to do with land, however. While most voices in the Israeli and international news media call on every Israeli prime minister to grant major concessions to the Palestinians, what should in fact happen is that Israel should apply sovereignty over the Jewish communities of Judea and Samaria. In the Knesset, in 2011, I introduced the Annexation for Declaration Initiative, which calls for Israel to annex the areas of Judea and Samaria where Jewish communities reside. Numerous Knesset members from across the political spectrum have since declared their support for this plan.

Talks on the establishment of a Palestinian state must cease, effective immediately. Next, Israel should declare its right to exist within current borders without further surrender of territory. Any threat to Israel and its citizens will be eliminated with dispatch. All of the diplomatic and security assistance that Israel provides to the Palestinians must be halted, and the transfer of tax revenues—upward of $1 billion per year—must end until Palestinians demonstrably stop the incitement and terrorist attacks. This alone could threaten the very existence of the Palestinian Authority.

Second, any future U.N. vote on Palestinian statehood would give Israel an opportunity to annex all of the Jewish communities in Judea and Samaria, as we did with the eastern half of Jerusalem and with the Golan Heights. We could, in the future, extend full Israeli jurisdiction to the Jewish communities and uninhabited lands of Judea and Samaria. This would put an end to a legal limbo that has existed since 1967. Our goal is to have the majority of the land in Judea and Samaria with a minimum number of Palestinians, which includes Jewish communities and the vacant land. We would not annex those areas heavily populated with Palestinians. What we would do is to offer Palestinians linkage and connection between Palestinian towns, where they would be able to travel freely from place to place without being stopped by roadblocks. They would have complete self-rule. As for civil issues, different regional centers would run the daily civic life of the Palestinians. The local leader in Hebron, Sheik Abu Bakr Gabry, is supportive of this idea. He is on the ground and in charge of a major area. The permanent status of Palestinians would be determined in the final peace agreement, which would be signed with Jordan and Egypt. There would be no connection or linkage between Gaza and Judea and Samaria.

In addition to its obvious ideological and symbolic significance, legalizing our hold on Judea and Samaria would also increase the security of all Israelis by depriving terrorists of a base and creating a buffer zone against threats from the east. Moreover, we would be well within our rights to assert, as we did in Gaza after our disengagement in 2005, that we are no longer responsible for the Palestinian residents of the West Bank, who would continue to live in their own un-annexed towns. While naysayers will no doubt warn us of the dire consequences and international condemnation that are sure to follow such a move by Israel, this would not be the first time that Israel has made such controversial decisions.

In 1949, Prime Minister David Ben-Gurion moved the Knesset to Jerusalem and declared it the capital of the State of Israel despite the 1947 United Nations partition plan, which had designated the city an international zone. Immediately after the 1967 Six-Day War, Prime Minister Levi Eshkol annexed East Jerusalem and declared that the city would remain a united and undivided entity. And in 1981, Prime Minister Menachem Begin extended Israeli sovereignty to the Golan Heights. In each of these cases, Israel's actions were met with harsh international criticism and threats of sanctions; all of these decisions, however, are cornerstones of today's reality.

Our leaders made these decisions based on the realization that their actions would further Zionist values and strengthen the State of Israel. The diplomatic storms soon blew over as the international community moved on to other issues. It would be wise of any Israeli prime minister to follow in their footsteps.

In fact, if the Palestinians decide they want to end the Oslo agreements and begin experimenting with unilateral actions, then an unexpected opening will present itself for Israel. Our leaders must seize this opportunity and right a historic wrong by applying Israeli sovereignty, annexing parts of our homeland.

As for refugees, even the Palestinians understand that they all cannot come into Israel. On December 11, 1948, the U.N. General Assembly resolved: "that refugees wishing to return to their homes and live at peace with their neighbour should be permitted to do so at the earliest practicable date."[22] This resolution has been re-affirmed by the General Assembly yearly, but General Assembly resolutions are non-binding and Israel argues correctly that the "live in peace" condition has never been met. In addition, consider that 1,951,603 Palestinian refugees are located in Jordan, out of which 338,000 still live in refugee camps, the only goal of which is both to keep the refugee issue alive and because Jordan is very afraid of a Palestinian majority.[23]

In fact, even Palestinians understand that they are not capable of repatriating one hundred percent. During negotiations the Palestinians have asked for a symbolic number, perhaps a few thousand a year, who would come back. They must understand that they left their old life the same way Jews left Arab nations like Iraq, Iran, Lebanon, Tunisia, Libya, and Algeria. When they moved they understood that they would not be returning. They left businesses and homes and many assets that were overtaken by the remaining populations. We need to remember that even if there is a right of return, which I do not recognize, we are talking only about those who left their homes and not future generations. That number, because of the age factor, is getting smaller and smaller. Still, there are people and organizations who enjoy making a living out of the so-called refugee issue.

Finally, incitement and the teaching of hatred must stop—it will take years for this to have an impact, which is why it is so important for it to stop as soon as possible. So much damage has already been done. Remember that there are generations of people who have been taught hatred. Think of this—in March 2011 *teenagers* slaughtered the sleeping Udi and Ruth Fogel and three of their children, including three-month-old baby Hadas. Hakim Maazan Niad Awad, 18, and Amjad Mahmed Fauzi Awad, 19, were arrested for the crime, and later convicted. Hakim Awad was a high school student who has been linked to the Popular Front for the Liberation of Palestine group in the Samarian village of Awarta. These boys were born just a year or so after the Oslo accord was signed. You ask how such young people can get to a point where they can knife small, sleeping children and babies to death. They are not insane; the boys grew up in an average village and received a standard Palestinian education, which includes intense lessons in hatred and anti-Semitism. For instance, according to news reports, Hakim's father, Maazan, is a PFLP member who served five years in a Palestinian Authority prison in the late 1990s for the murder of a female cousin and the burning of her body. Hakim's uncle, Jibril Awad, was a PFLP member who transported a terrorist to Itamar, a Jewish community, in 2002 on a Friday night. In that attack, Rahel Shabu, her three sons, and resident Yosef Twitto were shot and killed.[24]

While this is depraved and shocking, it is not surprising. The fact that Mahmoud Abbas, current chairman of the Palestinian Authority, met with the terrorist Amina Muna on December 2011 in Turkey tells us much about who is leading the Palestinians. Muna is a Palestinian woman who lured Israeli teenager Ofir

Nahum to his death through an Internet flirtation, and was sentenced to life in 2003 by an Israeli military court. She spent time trolling chat rooms to find a potential victim and found Nahum at random. Muna gave Nahum a fake identity, telling him that she was a new immigrant to Israel, and she convinced him to meet her in Jerusalem. They met and Muna took him in a cab to Ramallah, a ten-minute drive away. There were a group of terrorists waiting for them and they killed him.

Muna became a symbol for Palestinians, and in jail she became a leader. She never regretted for a moment what she had done, and in fact is very proud of the fact that she was able to contribute to the murder of an innocent Israeli. The fact that this woman should be idolized is a tragedy but indicative of the problem we face in the peace process. She was one of the more than 1,000 terrorists released in the Gilad Shalit prisoner exchange in October 2011. How can Israel be expected to sit at a negotiating table with someone who promotes the murder of children by paying respect to such an evildoer? The Palestinians see this move as a sign that the kind of activity Muna was engaged in is not just acceptable, but encouraged.

LONG-TERM GOALS AND THE
THREE-STATE SOLUTION

What I am proposing here is a three-state solution. This would entail a regional agreement with Jordan, Egypt, and Israel that would give Palestinians land and other rights across these three areas— not land to form a distinct Palestinian state but land within the borders of these states as they exist now. Clearly peace can only be achieved through partnership between these regional countries. Difficult yes; impossible no. Had I said to you a few years ago that

Hamas would control Gaza, and that an Arab Spring would bring about major protests and upheaval and the overthrow of well-entrenched strong-arm governments, you would have called me a lunatic. Yet it is happening. So we know that anything is possible.

The implementation of this annexation plan, followed by full sovereignty, is imperative to ensure that Israel's borders, citizens, and livelihood remains safe and secure. Israel and its neighbors, including Egypt and Jordan, will jointly bear the costs of accommodating the Palestinian issue.

Before we can make the three-state solution a reality, there needs to be two pre-conditions. The first, as I said earlier, would be real recognition by all in the region that Israel has a right to exist. Second, in order to be victorious, Israel must take on and defeat those who are against us—Hamas, Hezbollah, and others. We cannot negotiate or work toward peace as long as these entities exist.

Palestinians already constitute 70 percent of Jordan's population, and they actively participate in all aspects of the country. They hold positions in political office, prosper economically, and are socially adept. Since 1950, approximately half of Jordan's prime ministers have been Arab Palestinians. King Abdullah of Jordan in 1948 claimed, "Palestine and Jordan are one." Again in 1981, King Hussein stated, "the truth is that Jordan is Palestine and Palestine is Jordan."

Egypt has also shown its support for the Palestinians by playing a crucial role in supporting their government over the years. With the reopening of the Rafah border crossing to Gaza and continued public expressions of support, Egypt has become increasingly pro-Palestinian. In fact, Palestinians living in Egypt have been granted residency with the right to work and travel. They also receive education subsidies and enjoy the advantages of Egyptian citizens while maintaining their Palestinian identity.

Given these facts, I do not think it is unreasonable to ask both Jordan and Egypt to play their part in bringing lasting security to the region by embracing the three-state solution, enabling the region to finally live in peace and prosper economically and socially. I believe it is possible to make both countries understand that a separate Palestinian state would be dangerous for them as well, and it is in their interests to work toward a three-state solution.

First let me make it clear that this plan is not going to happen tomorrow. Perhaps this is why it's not an idea that has taken hold with American presidents and others who have an interest in getting things done quickly and with fanfare. They have to realize that the Middle East is on a different timeline. To make change in the region, things must be done slowly over time. Politically, it's hard to imagine the plan because it's not the kind of thing that will happen in four years so that an American president can take credit for it in his or her term. As I said earlier, a strong will and powerful arguments can and will make progress in time.

The remaining enclaves of Palestinian towns and villages would either be self-ruled or be part of Jordan or Egypt. I, and all Israelis, want to see Palestinians live freely and independently with no intervention by Israel whatsoever, but linked to Jordan, Egypt, and other areas in the Middle East. They could import and export whatever they needed to in terms of economic development. I would hope that they thrive on their own, because the better off people are, the less likely they will be prone to violence and terrorism.

Palestinians living in Judea and Samaria have done quite well economically. Over the past five years, Palestinian real GDP there has risen by about a third, to almost $8.1 billion in 2010. The number of private sector jobs has risen by more than 78,000 and the number of companies listed on the Palestinian stock market has increased significantly from 28 in 2005 to 45 in 2011. Dependency on international aid has fallen from over $1.8 billion in 2008 to about $1.1 billion in 2010. Judea/Samaria has seen an increase in GDP per capita of almost 50 percent. International recognition of the improving economy has also grown, with foreign direct investment climbing from $18.6 million in 2006 to $264.5 million in 2009.[25]

However, security remains an issue and continues to be a reminder of why a Palestinian state would not work. Case in point is the Erez Industrial Zone, a joint Israeli, Palestinian, and Arab project that started in 1970, three years after Israel took over Gaza in the Six-Day War. The project began when the PLO was still universally recognized as a terror organization. The project exemplified Israeli optimism and success in working together with the Palestinian Arab population under Israeli control. It also provided thousands of jobs for Gazans—jobs that did not exist when they were under Egyptian control. It was, economically and socially, good for everyone. By 2001, there were 187 businesses at Erez,[26] from carpentry shops to metal works, employing more than 5,000 Arabs who made a good living that provided well for their families.

Then, starting in 2001, Hamas and Islamic Jihad targeted this successful symbol of cooperation and peace. Between 2001 and 2004, at least 11 Israelis were killed at Erez by terror attacks. In four years, Palestinian terror networks targeted the Erez Crossing with almost 500 mortar shells. Companies found it increasingly difficult to keep their businesses open while providing a safe environment for their employees. Millions of dollars were lost because of the terror attacks. In 2004, the Israeli government announced that it could no longer keep the industrial area open, and all Israeli companies withdrew. In the intervening years Erez has fallen into disuse because of continuing terror. In May 2008, a Palestinian bomber from Gaza blew up an explosives-laden truck on the

Palestinian side of the Erez Crossing, causing an estimated $3.5 million in damages to the Israeli checkpoint.[27] The same people who were responsible for the destruction at Erez now control Gaza.

ISRAEL AND THE WORLD

If the statistics are right, the Jews constitute but one percent of the human race. It suggests a nebulous dim puff of smoke lost in the blaze of the Milky Way. Properly the Jew ought hardly to be heard of; but he is heard of, has always been heard of. He is as prominent on the planet as any other people, and his commercial importance is extravagantly out of proportion to the smallness of his bulk. His contributions to the world's list of great names in literature, science, art, music, finance, medicine, and abstruse learning, are also way out of proportion to the weakness of his numbers. He has made a marvelous fight in this world, in all ages: and has done it with his hands tied behind him. All things are mortal but the Jew; all other forces pass, but he remains. What is the secret of his immortality?[28]

—Mark Twain

Israel is the one hundredth smallest country in the world, home to less than 1/1000th of the world's population with just 7.1 million people. Its $100 billion economy is larger than all of its immediate neighbors combined. Israel has the highest average living standards in the Middle East. Israel has the highest number of university degrees per capita among working people, ranking third in the industrialized world after the United States and Holland. It also has the highest number of museums, orchestras, and zoos per capita. Israel produces more scientific papers per capita than any other nation by a large margin—109 per 10,000 people—and also has one of the highest per capita rates of patents filed.

As chronicled in Saul Singer and Dan Senor's *New York Times* bestseller, *Start-Up Nation: The Story of Israel's Economic Miracle,* Israel is the birthplace of numerous technological advancements, including the cell phone, which was developed in Israel by Israelis working in the Israeli branch of Motorola. Most of the Windows NT and XP operating systems were developed by Microsoft-Israel. The Pentium MMX Chip technology was designed in Israel at Intel. Both the PentiuM-4 microprocessor and the Centrino processor were entirely designed, developed, and produced in Israel. The Pentium microprocessor in your computer was most likely made in Israel. Voice mail technology was developed in Israel. The technology for the AOL Instant Messenger ICQ was developed in 1996 by four young Israelis. According to industry officials, Israel designed the airline industry's most impenetrable flight security. U.S. officials now look to Israel for advice on how to handle airborne security threats.

In proportion to its population, Israel has the largest number of startup companies in the world. In absolute terms, Israel has more startup companies than any other country in the world, except the United States. With more than 3,000 high-tech companies and startups, Israel has the highest concentration of high-tech companies in the world—apart from Silicon Valley. Israel is ranked number two in the world for venture capital funds, right behind the United States. Outside the United States and Canada, Israel has the largest number of NASDAQ-listed companies.

Why are these achievements—which only scratch the surface of the marvelous ingenuity of Israelis—so important to review? Because all of this creative innovative energy is expended to the world's benefit against a backdrop of unrelenting wars with a relentless enemy that seeks Israel's destruction. Our economy is continuously under strain because of our defense expenditures. Still, the Israeli people do not let these difficulties undermine their entrepreneurial and intellectual pursuits and talents. What springs from our minds and hands is more valuable, ultimately, than all the oil in the world. What more could come from my tiny country if we didn't have to continuously defend ourselves from terrorists and enemies? Our motives are to live in peace—our developments in science, the arts, and technology prove it. I hope I've made the case that we must defend ourselves without question, and by acting in our best interests we are, in fact, acting in the interests of the civilized, modern, liberal world. We have the will and with that will we will prevail.

> The LORD will give strength unto His people;
> the LORD will bless his people with peace
>
> —Psalms 29:11

APPENDIX A

GENERAL PROVISIONS OSLO ACCORDS

1. The permanent status of the territories will be negotiated "as soon as possible." Negotiations will commence within two years, and will be completed within five years. Subjects to be discussed will include Jerusalem, refugees, settlements and boundaries.
2. The Palestinian Interim Council will have no authority over Jerusalem, settlements, military locations or Israelis.
3. The Council will have jurisdiction, including legislative power, over education, culture, health, welfare, direct taxation and tourism. Separate Palestinian "Authorities" will act in co-ordination with Israel to deal with water, environment, electricity, ports, banking etc.
4. Israel will retain jurisdiction over external security, foreign affairs and Israeli citizens, as well as all other powers not specifically transferred to the Council.
5. Israeli-Palestinian liaison committees will be established, and co-operation and assistance will be sought from Jordan and Egypt.
6. Detailed provisions were made for economic development programs, including finance by the major economic powers, and

by Arab sources, for joint Jordanian-Israeli development of the Dead Sea and a possible Mediterranean–Dead Sea Canal, the development of a major port in Gaza, and general infra-structure, including roads, railways, communication lines etc.

APPENDIX B

THE COUNCIL OF THE LEAGUE OF NATIONS

WHEREAS THE PRINCIPAL ALLIED POWERS HAVE AGREED, FOR THE PUR-pose of giving effect to the provisions of Article 22 of the Covenant of the League of Nations, to entrust to a Mandatory selected by the said Powers the administration of the territory of Palestine, which formerly belonged to the Turkish Empire, within such boundaries as may be fixed by them; and

Whereas the Principal Allied Powers have also agreed that the Mandatory should be responsible for putting into effect the declaration originally made on November 2nd, 1917, by the Government of His Britannic Majesty, and adopted by the said Powers, in favour of the establishment in Palestine of a national home for the Jewish people, it being clearly understood that nothing should be done which might prejudice the civil and religious rights of existing non-Jewish communities in Palestine, or the rights and political status enjoyed by Jews in any other country; and

Whereas recognition has thereby been given to the historical connection of the Jewish people with Palestine and to the grounds for reconstituting their national home in that country; and

Whereas the Principal Allied Powers have selected His Britannic Majesty as the Mandatory for Palestine; and

Whereas the mandate in respect of Palestine has been formulated in the following terms and submitted to the Council of the League for approval; and

Whereas His Britannic Majesty has accepted the mandate in respect of Palestine and undertaken to exercise it on behalf of the League of Nations in conformity with the following provisions; and

Whereas by the afore-mentioned Article 22 (paragraph 8), it is provided that the degree of authority, control or administration to be exercised by the Mandatory, not having been previously agreed upon by the Members of the League, shall be explicitly defined by the Council of the League of Nations;

Confirming the said mandate, defines its terms as follows:

ARTICLE 1.

The Mandatory shall have full powers of legislation and of administration, save as they may be limited by the terms of this mandate.

ARTICLE 2.

The Mandatory shall be responsible for placing the country under such political, administrative and economic conditions as will secure the establishment of the Jewish national home, as laid down in the preamble, and the development of self-governing institutions, and also for safeguarding the civil and religious rights of all the inhabitants of Palestine, irrespective of race and religion.

ARTICLE 3.

The Mandatory shall, so far as circumstances permit, encourage local autonomy.

ARTICLE 4.

An appropriate Jewish agency shall be recognised as a public body for the purpose of advising and co-operating with the Administration of Palestine in such economic, social and other matters as may affect the establishment of the Jewish national home and the interests of the Jewish population in Palestine, and, subject always to the control of the Administration, to assist and take part in the development of the country.

The Zionist organisation, so long as its organisation and constitution are in the opinion of the Mandatory appropriate, shall be recognised as such agency. It shall take steps in consultation with His Britannic Majesty's Government to secure the co-operation of all Jews who are willing to assist in the establishment of the Jewish national home.

ARTICLE 5.

The Mandatory shall be responsible for seeing that no Palestine territory shall be ceded or leased to, or in any way placed under the control of, the Government of any foreign Power.

ARTICLE 6.

The Administration of Palestine, while ensuring that the rights and position of other sections of the population are not prejudiced, shall facilitate Jewish immigration under suitable conditions and shall encourage, in co-operation with the Jewish agency. referred to in Article 4, close settlement by Jews, on the land, including State lands and waste lands not required for public purposes.

ARTICLE 7.

The Administration of Palestine shall be responsible for enacting a nationality law. There shall be included in this law provisions framed so as to facilitate the acquisition of Palestinian citizenship by Jews who take up their permanent residence in Palestine.

ARTICLE 8.

The privileges and immunities of foreigners, including the benefits of consular jurisdiction and protection as formerly enjoyed by Capitulation or usage in the Ottoman Empire, shall not be applicable in Palestine.

Unless the Powers whose nationals enjoyed the afore-mentioned privileges and immunities on August 1st, 1914, shall have previously renounced the right to their re-establishment, or shall have agreed to their non-application for a specified period, these privileges and immunities shall, at the expiration of the mandate, be immediately re-established in their entirety or with such modifications as may have been agreed upon between the Powers concerned.

ARTICLE 9.

The Mandatory shall be responsible for seeing that the judicial system established in Palestine shall assure to foreigners, as well as to natives, a complete guarantee of their rights.

Respect for the personal status of the various peoples and communities and for their religious interests shall be fully guaranteed. In particular, the control and administration of Wakfs shall be exercised in accordance with religious law and the dispositions of the founders.

ARTICLE 10.

Pending the making of special extradition agreements relating to Palestine, the extradition treaties in force between the Mandatory and other foreign Powers shall apply to Palestine.

ARTICLE 11.

The Administration of Palestine shall take all necessary measures to safeguard the interests of the community in connection with the development of the country, and, subject to any international obligations accepted by the Mandatory, shall have full power to provide for public ownership or control of any of the natural resources of the country or of the public works, services and utilities established or to be established therein. It shall introduce a land system appropriate to the needs of the country, having regard, among other things, to the desirability of promoting the close settlement and intensive cultivation of the land.

The Administration may arrange with the Jewish agency mentioned in Article 4 to construct or operate, upon fair and equitable terms, any public works, services and utilities, and to develop any of the natural resources of the country, in so far as these matters are not directly undertaken by the Administration. Any such arrangements shall provide that no profits distributed by such agency, directly or indirectly, shall exceed a reasonable rate of interest on the capital, and any further profits shall be utilised by it for the benefit of the country in a manner approved by the Administration.

ARTICLE 12.

The Mandatory shall be entrusted with the control of the foreign relations of Palestine and the right to issue exequaturs to consuls appointed by foreign Powers. He shall also be entitled to afford diplomatic and consular protection to citizens of Palestine when outside its territorial limits.

ARTICLE 13.

All responsibility in connection with the Holy Places and religious buildings or sites in Palestine, including that of preserving existing rights and of securing free access to the Holy Places, religious buildings and sites and the free exercise of worship, while ensuring the requirements of public order and decorum, is assumed by the Mandatory, who shall be responsible solely to the League of Nations in all matters connected herewith, provided that nothing in this article shall prevent the Mandatory from entering into such arrangements as he may deem reasonable with the Administration for the purpose of carrying the provisions of this article into effect; and provided also that nothing in this mandate shall be construed as conferring upon the Mandatory authority to interfere with the fabric or the management of purely Moslem sacred shrines, the immunities of which are guaranteed.

ARTICLE 14.

A special Commission shall be appointed by the Mandatory to study, define and determine the rights and claims in connection with the Holy Places and the rights and claims relating to the different religious communities in Palestine. The method of nomination, the composition and the functions of this Commission shall be submitted to the Council of the League for its approval, and the Commission shall not be appointed or enter upon its functions without the approval of the Council.

ARTICLE 15.

The Mandatory shall see that complete freedom of conscience and the free exercise of all forms of worship, subject only to the maintenance of public order and morals, are ensured to all. No discrimination of any kind shall be made between the inhabitants of Palestine on the ground of race, religion or language. No person shall be excluded from Palestine on the sole ground of his religious belief.

The right of each community to maintain its own schools for the education of its own members in its own language, while conforming to such educational requirements of a general nature as the Administration may impose, shall not be denied or impaired.

ARTICLE 16.

The Mandatory shall be responsible for exercising such supervision over religious or eleemosynary bodies of all faiths in Palestine as may be required for the maintenance of public order and good government. Subject to such supervision, no measures shall be taken in Palestine to obstruct or interfere with the enterprise of such bodies or to discriminate against any representative or member of them on the ground of his religion or nationality.

ARTICLE 17.

The Administration of Palestine may organise on a voluntary basis the forces necessary for the preservation of peace and order, and also for the defence of the country, subject, however, to the supervision of the Mandatory, but shall not use them for purposes other than those above specified save with the consent of the Mandatory. Except for such purposes, no military, naval or air forces shall be raised or maintained by the Administration of Palestine.

Nothing in this article shall preclude the Administration of Palestine from contributing to the cost of the maintenance of the forces of the Mandatory in Palestine.

The Mandatory shall be entitled at all times to use the roads, railways and ports of Palestine for the movement of armed forces and the carriage of fuel and supplies.

ARTICLE 18.

The Mandatory shall see that there is no discrimination in Palestine against the nationals of any State Member of the League of Nations (including companies incorporated under its laws) as compared with those of the Mandatory or of any foreign State in matters concerning taxation, commerce or navigation, the exercise of industries or professions, or in the treatment of merchant vessels or civil aircraft. Similarly, there shall be no discrimination in Palestine against goods originating in or destined for any of the said States, and there shall be freedom of transit under equitable conditions across the mandated area.

Subject as aforesaid and to the other provisions of this mandate, the Administration of Palestine may, on the advice of the Mandatory, impose such taxes and customs duties as it may consider necessary, and take such steps as it may think best to promote the development of the natural resources of the country and to safeguard the interests of the population. It may also, on the advice of the Mandatory, conclude a special customs agreement with any State the territory of which in 1914 was wholly included in Asiatic Turkey or Arabia.

ARTICLE 19.

The Mandatory shall adhere on behalf of the Administration of Palestine to any general international conventions already existing, or which may be concluded hereafter with the approval of the League of Nations, respecting the slave traffic, the traffic in arms and ammunition, or the traffic in drugs, or relating to commercial equality, freedom of transit and navigation, aerial navigation and postal, telegraphic and wireless communication or literary, artistic or industrial property.

ARTICLE 20.

The Mandatory shall co-operate on behalf of the Administration of Palestine, so far as religious, social and other conditions may permit, in the execution of any common policy adopted by the League of Nations for preventing and combating disease, including diseases of plants and animals.

ARTICLE 21.

The Mandatory shall secure the enactment within twelve months from this date, and shall ensure the execution of a Law of Antiquities based on the following rules. This law shall ensure equality of treatment in the matter of excavations and archaeological research to the nations of all States Members of the League of Nations.

(1) "Antiquity" means any construction or any product of human activity earlier than the year A.D. 1700.

(2) The law for the protection of antiquities shall proceed by encouragement rather than by threat.

Any person who, having discovered an antiquity without being furnished with the authorisation referred to in paragraph 5, reports the same to an official of the competent Department, shall be rewarded according to the value of the discovery.

(3) No antiquity may be disposed of except to the competent Department, unless this Department renounces the acquisition of any such antiquity.

No antiquity may leave the country without an export licence from the said Department.

(4) Any person who maliciously or negligently destroys or damages an antiquity shall be liable to a penalty to be fixed.

(5) No clearing of ground or digging with the object of finding antiquities shall be permitted, under penalty of fine, except to persons authorised by the competent Department.

(6) Equitable terms shall be fixed for expropriation, temporary or permanent, of lands which might be of historical or archaeological interest.

(7) Authorisation to excavate shall only be granted to persons who show sufficient guarantees of archaeological experience. The Administration of Palestine shall not, in granting these authorisations, act in such a way as to exclude scholars of any nation without good grounds.

(8) The proceeds of excavations may be divided between the excavator and the competent Department in a proportion fixed by that Department. If division seems impossible for scientific reasons, the excavator shall receive a fair indemnity in lieu of a part of the find.

ARTICLE 22.

English, Arabic and Hebrew shall be the official languages of Palestine. Any statement or inscription in Arabic on stamps or money in Palestine shall be repeated in Hebrew, and any statement or inscription in Hebrew shall be repeated in Arabic.

ARTICLE 23.

The Administration of Palestine shall recognise the holy days of the respective communities in Palestine as legal days of rest for the members of such communities.

ARTICLE 24.

The Mandatory shall make to the Council of the League of Nations an annual report to the satisfaction of the Council as to the measures taken during the year to carry out the provisions of the mandate. Copies of all laws and regulations promulgated or issued during the year shall be communicated with the report.

ARTICLE 25.

In the territories lying between the Jordan and the eastern boundary of Palestine as ultimately determined, the Mandatory shall be entitled, with the consent of the Council of the League of Nations, to postpone or withhold application of such provisions of this mandate as he may consider inapplicable to the existing local conditions, and to make such provision for the administration of the territories as he may consider suitable to those conditions, provided that no action shall be taken which is inconsistent with the provisions of Articles 15, 16 and 18.

ARTICLE 26.

The Mandatory agrees that, if any dispute whatever should arise between the Mandatory and another Member of the League of Nations relating to the interpretation or the application of the provisions of the mandate, such dispute, if it cannot be settled by negotiation, shall be submitted to the Permanent Court of International Justice provided for by Article 14 of the Covenant of the League of Nations.

ARTICLE 27.

The consent of the Council of the League of Nations is required for any modification of the terms of this mandate.

ARTICLE 28.

In the event of the termination of the mandate hereby conferred upon the Mandatory, the Council of the League of Nations shall make such arrangements as may be deemed necessary for safeguarding in perpetuity, under guarantee of the League, the rights secured by Articles 13 and 14, and shall use its influence for securing, under the guarantee of the League, that the Government of Palestine will fully honour the financial obligations legitimately incurred by the Administration of Palestine during the period of the mandate, including the rights of public servants,to pensions or gratuities.

The present instrument shall be deposited in original in the archives of the League of Nations and certified copies shall be forwarded by the Secretary-General of the League of Nations to all Members of the League.

Done at London the twenty-fourth day of July,
one thousand nine hundred and twenty-two.

APPENDIX C

RESOLUTION 242

OPERATIVE PARAGRAPH ONE "AFFIRMS THAT THE FULFILLMENT OF Charter principles requires the establishment of a just and lasting peace in the Middle East which should include the application of both the following principles:

(i) Withdrawal of Israel armed forces from territories occupied in the recent conflict;

(ii) Termination of all claims or states of belligerency and respect for and acknowledgment of the sovereignty, territorial integrity and political independence of every State in the area and their right to live in peace within secure and recognized boundaries free from threats or acts of force."[1]

APPENDIX D

BIBLICAL CONNECTIONS TO ISRAEL AND JERUSALEM

THE FOLLOWING ARE JUST SOME OF THE PA   SSAGES FROM THE BIBLE that indicate that Jerusalem is part of Israel.

> GENESIS 12:7A: "The Lord appeared to Abram and said, 'To your descendants I will give this land.'"
>
> GENESIS 13:15: ". . . for all the land which you see, I will give it to you and to your descendants forever."
>
> GENESIS 15:18: "To your descendants I have given this land."
>
> GENESIS 17:7–8: "And I will establish My covenant between Me and you and your descendants after you throughout their generations for an everlasting covenant, to be God to you and to your descendants after you. And I will give to you and to your descendants after you, the land of your sojourning, all the land of Canaan, for an everlasting possession; and I will be their God."
>
> JEREMIAH 31:35–36: "This is what the Lord says, 'He who appoints the sun to shine by day, Who decrees the moon and stars to shine by night,

Who stirs up the sea so that its waves roar—the Lord Almighty is His Name; Only if these ordinances vanish from My sight,' declares the Lord, 'will the descendants of Israel ever cease to be a nation before Me.'"

GENESIS 12:1–3: "The Lord has said to Abram, 'Leave your country, your people and your father's household and go to the land I will show you. I will make you into a great nation and I will bless you; I will make your name great, and you will be a blessing. I will bless those who bless you and whoever curses you I will curse; and all the peoples on earth will be blessed through you."

GENESIS 17:18: Abraham said to God, "Oh that Ishmael might live before Thee." In Genesis 17:19, God answered Abraham: "No, but Sarah your wife shall bear you a son, and you shall call his name Isaac; and I will establish My covenant with him for an everlasting covenant for his descendants after him."

GENESIS 28:13–15: "I am the Lord, the God of your father Abraham and the God of Isaac; the land on which you lie, I will give it to you and to your descendants. Your descendants shall also be like the dust of the earth, and you shall spread out to the west and to the east and to the north and to the south; and in you and in your descendants shall all the families of the earth be blessed. And behold, I am with you, and will keep you wherever you go, and will bring you back to this land; for I will not leave you until I have done what I have promised you."

DEUTERONOMY 1:8: "See, I have placed the land before you; go in and possess the land which the Lord swore to give to your fathers, to Abraham, to Isaac, and to Jacob, to them and their descendants after them."

JOSHUA 1:2–4,6: "Moses My servant is dead. Now then, you and all these people, get ready to cross the Jordan river into the land I am about to give to them—to the Israelites. I will give you every place where you set your foot, as I promised Moses. Your territory will extend from the desert and from Lebanon to the great river, the Euphrates—all the Hittite country—and to the Great Sea on the west. Be strong and courageous, because you will lead these people to inherit the land I swore to their forefathers to give them."

LEVITICUS 26:44–45: "Yet in spite of this, when they are in the land of their enemies, I will not reject them, nor will I so abhor them as to destroy them, breaking My covenant with them; for I am the Lord their God. But I will remember for them the covenant with their ancestors, whom I brought out of the land of Egypt in the sight of the nations, that I might be their God. I am the Lord."

DEUTERONOMY 30:3–5: "Then the Lord your God will restore you from captivity, and have compassion on you, and will gather you again from all the peoples where the Lord your God has scattered you. If your outcasts are at the ends of the earth, from there the Lord your God will gather you, and from there He will bring you back. And the Lord your God will bring you into the land which your fathers possessed, and you shall possess it; and He will prosper you and multiply you more than your fathers."

AMOS 9:14–15: "Also I will restore the captivity of My people Israel, and they will rebuild the ruined cities and live in them. They will also plant vineyards and drink their wine, and make gardens and eat their fruit. I will also plant them on their land, and they will not again be rooted out from their land which I have given them, says the Lord your God."

EZEKIEL 36:24: "I will take you from the nations and gather you from all the countries and bring you to your land."

EZEKIEL 37:11–12: "Then He said to me, 'Son of man, these bones are the whole house of Israel; behold, they say, Our bones are dried up, and our hope has perished. We are completely cut off.' Therefore prophesy, and say to them, 'thus says the Lord God, Behold, I will open your graves and cause you to come up out of your graves, My people; and I will bring you into the land of Israel.'"

APPENDIX E

MAPS

Regional Map of the Middle East

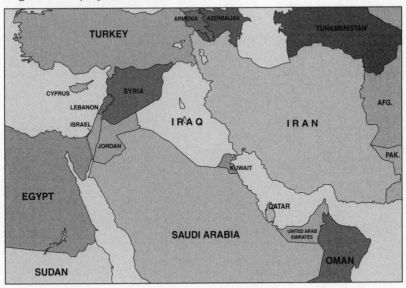

Map of Israel with Pre-1967 Borders

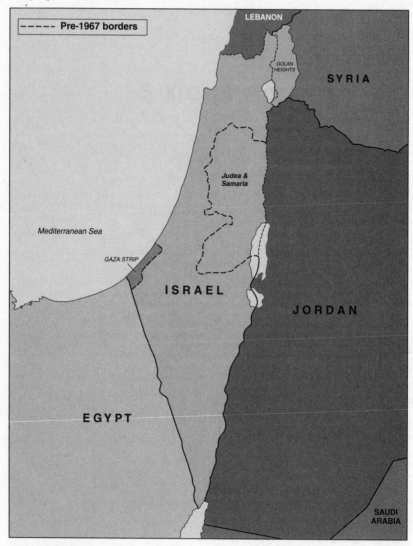

NOTES

INTRODUCTION: STANDING ON A PRECIPICE

1. No. 10-699 In the Supreme Court of the United States Menacham Binyamin Zivotofsky, by his Parents and Guardians Ari Z. and Naomi Siegman Zivotofsky, Petitioner v. Hillary Rodham Clinton, Secretary of State, viewed on December 15, 2011, <http://www.americanbar.org/content/dam/aba/publishing/previewbriefs/Other_Brief_Updates/10-699_respondent.authcheckdam.pdf>.
2. Mike Sacks, "Supreme Court Justice Ruth Bader Ginsberg Talks Constitution, Women, and Liberty on Egyptian TV (video)," Huffington Post, February 2, 2012, viewed on February 2, 2012, <http://www.huffingtonpost.com/2012/02/01/justice-ruth-bader-ginsburg-egypt_n_1248527.html>; Pamela Geller, "US Supreme Court Justice Ruth Bader Ginsburg to Egyptians: Look to the Constitutions of South Africa or Canada, Not to the US Constitution," Atlas Shrugged, February 2, 2012, viewed on February 2, 2012, <http://atlasshrugs2000.typepad.com/atlas_shrugs/2012/02/us-supreme-court-justice-ruth-bader-ginsburg-to-egyptians-look-to-the-constitutions-of-south-africa-.html>.

PART 1: DANGER AND OPPORTUNITY: THE CURRENT LANDSCAPE

1. Gavriel Queenann, "Gaza Economy Booming as Rockets Rain in Israel," Israel National News, December 8, 2011, viewed on December 15, 2011, <http://www.israelnationalnews.com/News/News.aspx/150546#.Tu9uJnORakk>.
2. The Religion of Peace website tracks terror attacks worldwide via a variety of news agencies and reports. As of March 2012, the number had reached 18,623. They provide sources for each attack reported. <http://www.religionofpeace.com>.
3. Jena Baker NcNeill, James Jay Carafano, Ph.D., and Jessica Zuckerman, "30 Terrorist Plots Foiled: How the System Worked," Heritage Foundation, April 29, 2010, viewed on December 15, 2011, <http://www.heritage.org/research/reports/2010/04/30-terrorist-plots-foiled-how-the-system-worked>.

4. Bernard Lewis, *The Political Language of Islam* (Chicago: University of Chicago Press, 1988), p. 72; Cf. William M. Watt, *Islamic Conceptions of the Holy War,* in Thomas P. Murphy, *The Holy War* (Columbus, OH: Ohio State University Press, 1974), p. 143.

5. Bernard Lewis, *The Crisis of Islam* (New York: The Modern Library, 2003), pp. 31-32.

6. A. E. Stahl, "'Offensive Jihad' in Sayyid Qutb's Ideology," International Institute for Counter-Terrorism, March 24, 2011, viewed on December 15, 2011, <http://www.ict.org.il/Articles/tabid/66/Articlsid/914/Default.aspx>.

7. Abdullah Azzam, "Defence of the Muslim Lands, The First Obligation after Iman," Religioscope, 2002, viewed on December 15, 2011, <http://www.religioscope.com/info/doc/jihad/azzam_defence_3_chap1.htm>.

8. Daniel Pipes, "Jihad through History," May 31, 2005, viewed on December 15, 2011, <http://www.danielpipes.org/2664/jihad-through-history>.

9. Paul Berman, *Terror and Liberalism* (New York: W.W. Norton & Co., 2004), p. 85.

10. Dale C. Eikmeier, "Qutbism: An Ideology of Islamic-Fascism," *Parameters* (spring 2007): pp. 85-98.

11. Fiona Symon, "Analysis: The Roots of Jihad," BBC News, October 16, 2001, viewed on January 2, 2012, <http://news.bbc.co.uk/2/hi/middle_east/1603178.stm>.

12. Asghar Schirazi, *The Constitution of Iran,* translated by John O'Kane (London: I.B. Tauris, 1998), p. 69.

13. Barry M. Rubin and Judith Colp Rubin, *Anti-American Terrorism and the Middle East: A Documentary Reader* (New York: Oxford University Press, 2004), p. 33.

14. Glenn Kessler, "Did Ahmadinejad Really Say Israel Should Be 'Wiped off the Map'?," *The Washington Post,* October 4, 2011, viewed on December 15, 2011, <http://www.washingtonpost.com/blogs/fact-checker/post/did-ahmadinejad-really-say-israel-should-be-wiped-off-the-map/2011/10/04/gIQABJIKML_blog.html>.

15. *Iran Foreign Policy and Government Guide, Volume I, Strategic Information and Policy* (Washington: International Business Publications, 2006), p. 143.

16. David Selbourne, *The Losing Battle with Islam* (New York: Prometheus Books, 2005), p. 31, p. 483.

17. John Irish, "Road to Radicalization from Toulouse to Kandahar," Reuters, March 21, 2012, viewed on March 21, 2012, <http://www.reuters.com/article/2012/03/21/us-france-shootings-suspect-idUSBRE82K1H420120321>.

18. Vincent Burns, Kate Dempsey Peterson, and James K. Kallstrom, *Terrorism: A Documentary and Reference Guide* (Santa Barbara: Greenwood Publishing Group, 2005), p. 232.

19. "King Abdullah: 'Israel Has an Expiration Date,'" Israel National News, November 21, 2011, viewed on December 16, 2011, <http://www.israelnationalnews.com/News/News.aspx/149968#.TvIqOnORakm>.

20. Antisemitic Incidents Reports Statistics and Trends, The Coordinating Forum for Countering Antisemitism, viewed on January 15, 2012, <http://antisemitism.org.il/list/4>.

21. "Tunisia: From 'Moderate Islam' to a 'Caliphate' in Three Weeks," *The Jewish Chronicle Online*, November 17, 2011, viewed on March 14, 2012, <http://www.thejc.com/blogs/alansimons/tunisia-from -moderate-islam-a-caliphate-three-weeks>.

22. "Israel and the Islamists," *The Economist*, December 10-16, 2011, p. 51.

23. Mahan Abedin, "Tunisia: The Advent of Liberal Islamism—An Interview with Rashid Al-Ghannouchi," New Age Islam, January 31, 2011, viewed on January 31, 2011, <http://www.newageislam.com /NewAgeIslamArticleDetail.aspx?ArticleID=4035>; Martin Kramer, "Rachid Ghannouchi: A Democrat within Islamism," Middle East Forum, fall 2002, viewed on December 15, 2011, <http://www.me forum.org/1492/rachid-ghannouchi-a-democrat-within-islamism>.

24. Jasmine Coleman, "Egypt Election Results Show Firm Win for Islamists," *The Guardian*, January 21, 2012, viewed January 21, 2012, <http://www .guardian.co.uk/world/2012/jan/21/egypt-election-clear-islamist -victory>.

25. For background on and history of the Muslim Brotherhood, see former assistant United States attorney Andrew C. McCarthy's well-argued *The Grand Jihad: How Islam and the Left Sabotage America* (New York: Encounter Books, 2010), and *The New Muslim Brotherhood in the West: A Comprehensive History of the Movement*, by Lorenzo Vidino (New York: Columbia University Press, 2010).

26. "Egyptian Uncertainties," *The Jerusalem Post*, November 24, 2011, viewed on December 16, 2011, <http://www.jpost.com/Opinion /Editorials/Article.aspx?id=246928>.

27. "Egyptians Embrace Revolt Leaders, Religious Parties and Military, As Well," Pew Research Global Attitudes Project, April 25, 2011, viewed December 17, 2011, <http://www.pewglobal.org/files/2011/04/Pew -Global-Attitudes-Egypt-Report-FINAL-April-25-2011.pdf>.

28. Yusri Mohamed, Sherine El Madany, and Ahmed Tolba, "Blast Hits Egypt's Gas Pipeline to Israel," Reuters, February 5, 2012, viewed February 5, 2012, <http://www.reuters.com/article/2012/02/05/egypt -gas-blast-idUSL5E8D40NQ20120205>.

29. Maggie Micheal and Hamza Hendawi, Associated Press, "Egypt Sends 43 NGO Workers to Trial over Funds," *The News Tribune*, <http:// www.thenewstribune.com/2012/02/04/2012477/death-toll-in -latest-egypt-clashes.html>.

30. All these dated examples are from "Islamic Terror Attacks on Christians (Since 9/11)," 2002-2012, viewed on January 16, 2012, <http://www .thereligionofpeace.com/Pages/ChristianAttacks.htm>.

31. Praveen Swami, "Mediator in Taliban-U.S. Talks Backed Kashmir Jihad," *The Hindu*, December 29, 2011, viewed on December 29, 2011, <http://www.thehindu.com/news/article2755817.ece>.

32. Mark Hosenball, Missy Ryan, and Warren Strobel, "U.S. Mulls Transfer of Taliban Prisoner in Perilous Peace Bid," Reuters, December 29, 2011, viewed on January 5, 2012, <http://ca.news.yahoo.com/exclusive-u -mulls-transfer-taliban-prisoner-perilous-233123630.html>.

33. David D. Kirkpatrick, "After Long Exile, Sunni Cleric Takes Role in Egypt," *The New York Times,* February 18, 2011, page A1, viewed on December 15, 2011, <http://www.nytimes.com/2011/02/19/world/middleeast/19egypt.html?pagewanted=all>.

34. "Yusuf al-Qaradawi," The Investigative Project on Terrorism, July 9, 2008, viewed on January 2, 2012, <http://www.investigativeproject.org/profile/167>.

35. Andrew McCarthy, "Obama Recruits Qaradawi," *National Review,* December 31, 2011, viewed December 31, 2011, <http://www.nationalreview.com/articles/286854/obama-recruits-qaradawi-andrew-c-mccarthy>.

36. "Sheikh Yousef Al-Qaradhawi on Al-Jazeera Incites against Jews, Arab Regimes, and the U.S.; Calls on Muslims to Boycott Starbucks and Others; Says 'Oh Allah, Take This Oppressive, Jewish, Zionist Band of People . . . And Kill Them, Down to the Very Last One,'" The Middle East Media Research Institute, January 12, 2009, viewed on January 5, 2012, <http://www.memri.org/report/en/0/0/0/0/0/0/3006.htm>.

37. Mark Landler, "Obama Got Message Supporting Talks with Taliban, but Maybe Not from Its Leader," *New York Times,* February 3, 2012, viewed on February 13, 2012, <http://www.nytimes.com/2012/02/04/world/asia/obama-got-letter-on-talks-maybe-from-taliban-leader.html>.

38. Graham E. Fuller, "Islamist Politics in Iraq after Saddam Hussein," United States Institute of Peace, August 2003, viewed January 5, 2012, <http://www.usip.org/publications/islamist-politics-iraq-after-saddam-hussein>.

39. Catherine Philp, "Iraq's Women of Power Who Tolerate Wife-Beating and Promote Polygamy," *The Times,* March 31, 2005, viewed on December 15, 2012, <http://www.chsbs.cmich.edu/fattah/courses/islampolitics/women.htm>.

40. Roi Kais, "Iraqi Bill to Ban Travel to Israel," YNet News, January 30, 2012, viewed January 30, 2012, <http://www.ynetnews.com/articles/0,7340,L-4182795,00.html>.

41. Roee Nahmias, contributor, "Hamas Mourns Bin Laden's Death," YNet News, February 5, 2011, viewed on December 16, 2011, <http://www.ynetnews.com/articles/0,7340,L-4063407,00.html>.

42. Karin Brulliard, "Hamas Ties to Syria and Iran in Flux as Region Shifts," *The Washington Post,* March 7, 2012, viewed on March 21, 2012, <http://www.washingtonpost.com/world/middle_east/hamas-ties-to-iran-in-flux-as-region-shifts/2012/03/06/gIQAhMvOxR_story.html>.

43. Barak Ravid, "Israel, Germany Plan Int'l Summit to Stop Iran Nuke Program," Haaretz.com, February 23, 2009, viewed on December 16, 2012, <http://www.haaretz.com/news/israel-germany-plan-int-l-summit-to-stop-iran-nuke-program-1.242054>.

44. Jay Solomon, "U.S. Woos Damascus by Easing Export Ban," *Wall Street Journal,* July 28, 2009, viewed on February 14, 2012, <http://online.wsj.com/article/SB124873789302385169.html>.

45. Bo Wilson, "Cameron and Obama Unite in Fresh Sanctions Threat to Syria," *London Evening Standard,* February 14, 2012, viewed on

February 14, 2012, <http://www.thisislondon.co.uk/standard/article
-24035228-cameron-and-obama-unite-in-fresh-sanctions-threat-to
-syria.do>.

46. Roger Cohen, "What Iran's Jews Say," February 22, 2009, viewed on December 16, 2012, <http://www.nytimes.com/2009/02/23/opinion/23cohen.html>.

47. Barbara Demick, "Iran: Life of Jews Living in Iran," Foundation for the Advancement of Sephardic Studies and Culture, viewed on December 16, 2012, <http://www.sephardicstudies.org/iran.html>.

48. Daniel Bettini, "Iran Executes Jewish Woman," YNet News, May 15, 2011, viewed on December 17, 2011, <http://www.ynetnews.com/articles/0,7340,L-4068646,00.html>.

49. Roger Cohen, <http://www.nytimes.com/2009/02/23/opinion/23cohen.html>.

50. Country Reports on Terrorism 2010, United States Department of State, viewed on January 15, 2012, <http://www.state.gov/documents/organization/170479.pdf>.

51. Reza Kahlili, "'Arab Spring' Part of Iranian Plot to Dominate," *American Thinker,* October 4, 2011, viewed on December 16, 2011, <http://www.americanthinker.com/2011/10/arab_spring_part_of_iranian_plot_to_dominate.html>.

52. IAEA Director General Yukiya Amano, "Introductory Statement to Board of Governors," November 17, 2011, viewed on March 15, 2012, <http://www.iaea.org/newscenter/statements/2011/amsp2011n030.html>.

53. Nicholas Blanford, "Hezbollah Waits and Prepares," *The Wall Street Journal,* November 19, 2011, viewed on January 5, 2012, <http://online.wsj.com/article/SB100014240529702036994045770441502779499624.html?KEYWORDS=%22iran%22>.

54. Mehdi Khalaji, "It's Time to Bypass Iran's 'Supreme Leader,'" *The Wall Street Journal,* February 9, 2012, viewed on February 9, 2012, <http://online.wsj.com/article/SB10001424052970204369404577206973232126642.html?mod=WSJ_Opinion_LEFTTopOpinion>.

55. Karl Vick and Aaron J. Klin, "Who Assassinated an Iranian Nuclear Scientist? Israel Isn't Telling," *Time,* January 13, 2012, viewed on January 13, 2012, <http://www.time.com/time/world/article/0,8599,2104372,00.html>.

56. Stephen Castle and Alan Cowell, "Europe and U.S. Tighten Vise of Sanctions on Iran," *The New York Times,* January 23, 2012, page A10, viewed on January 23, 2012, <http://www.nytimes.com/2012/01/24/world/middleeast/iran-urged-to-negotiate-as-west-readies-new-sanctions.html>.

57. "Iran Background," U.S. Energy Information Administration, November 2011, viewed on December 18, 2011, <http://www.eia.gov/countries/cab.cfm?fips=IR>.

58. "Treasury Designates Major Iranian State-Owned Bank," U.S. Department of the Treasury, January 23, 2012, viewed on January 24, 2012, <http://www.treasury.gov/press-center/press-releases/Pages/tg1397.aspx>.

59. Associated Press, "Deeper Iran Sanctions; US Targets Its Central Bank," February 6, 2012, viewed on February 6, 2012, <http://www.foxnews

.com/us/2012/02/06/us-levies-new-sanctions-on-irans-central
-bank/>.

60. "Iran," viewed on March 21, 2012, <http://www.webcitation.org/query
?id=1257023610265363>.

61. Mitchell D. Silber, "The Iranian Threat to New York City," *Wall Street
Journal*, February 14, 2012, viewed on February 14, 2012, <http:
//online.wsj.com/article/SB10001424052970203824904577215592376
556800.html?mod=WSJ_Opinion_LEADTop>.

62. Farnaz Fassihi, "Letter Writers Break Iranian Taboo," *Wall Street
Journal*, February 14, 2012, viewed on February 14, 2012, <http:
//online.wsj.com/article/SB10001424052970204642604577214420133
674482.html?KEYWORDS=iran+elections>.

63. "Russia: UN Report on Iran Nuclear Program Is Biased, Unprofessional,"
Haaretz.com, November 20, 2011, viewed on December 16, 2011,
<http://www.haaretz.com/news/diplomacy-defense/russia-un
-report-on-iran-nuclear-program-is-biased-unprofessional-1.3966
22>.

64. Iran's Oil Reserves, Global Security, viewed on December 18, 2011,
<http://www.globalsecurity.org/intell/world/iran/index.html>.

65. Melanie Lidman and Reuters, "US Calls New Construction in
J'lem 'Counterproductive,'" *The Jerusalem Post*, September 27,
2011, viewed on December 16, 2011, <http://www.jpost.com
/DiplomacyAndPolitics/Article.aspx?id=239776>.

66. "Obama Calls Israeli Settlement Building in East Jerusalem 'Dangerous,'"
Fox News, November 18, 2009, viewed on December 17, 2011, <http://
www.foxnews.com/politics/2009/11/18/obama-warns-double-dip
-recession/>.

67. "Quartet Urges Settlement Freeze," al-Jazeera, September 22, 2010,
viewed on December 16, 2011, <http://www.aljazeera.com/news
/middleeast/2010/09/2010921211511844268.html>.

68. David Lev, "Journalist Reveals the PA's 'Palestine Plot,'" Israel National
News, September 21-22, 2010, viewed on December 14, 2011, <http://
www.israelnationalnews.com/News/News.aspx/139742#.TsvqjnO
Rakk>.

69. Elad Benari, "Argentina, Uruguay Recognize PA as a State," Israel National
News, December 7, 2010, viewed on December 16, 2011, <http://
www.israelnationalnews.com/News/News.aspx/141023#.Tsvq23O
Rakk>.

70. "Daily Press Briefing," August 11, 2011, viewed on December 16, 2011,
<http://www.state.gov/r/pa/prs/dpb/2011/08/170420.htm>.

71. Mail Foreign Service, "Joe Biden's Snub to Netanyahu as He Arrives
90 Minutes Late for Dinner in Middle of Row with Israel over West
Bank Houses," Mail Online, March 10, 2010, viewed on December 16,
2011, <http://www.dailymail.co.uk/news/article-1256936/Joe-Biden
-snubs-Israeli-PM-surprise-announcement-build-homes-war-won
-land-U-S-vice-presidents-visit.html>.

72. Barak Ravid, "U.S. Warns Israel over Bill to Limit Foreign Funding to
NGOs," Haaretz.com, April 12, 2011, viewed on December 15, 2011,
<http://www.haaretz.com/news/diplomacy-defense/u-s-warns
-israel-over-bill-to-limit-foreign-funding-to-ngos-1.399442>.

73. Barak Ravid, "Government Ministers React Sharply to Clinton's Criticism of Israeli Democracy," Haaretz.com, April 12, 2011, viewed on December 17, 2011, <http://www.haaretz.com/news/diplomacy -defense/government-ministers-react-sharply-to-clinton-s-criticism -of-israeli-democracy-1.399450>.

74. Jamila Hussain, *Islam: Its Law and Society*, second edition (Australia: The Federation Press, 2003), p. 69; Kristin Deasy, "Bans, *burqinis* and bad *hijab*," *Asia Times*, November 18, 2009, viewed on January 16, 2012, <http://www.atimes.com/atimes/Middle_East/KK18Ak03.html>.

75. International Campaign for Human Rights in Iran, <http://www.iran humanrights.org/>.

76. Aviad Glickman, "High Court Rejects Cadet's Petition over Woman's Singing," October 5, 2011, viewed on February 5, 2012, <http://www .ynetnews.com/articles/0,7340,L-4131833,00.html>.

77. Herb Keinon, "Erdogan Threatens to Send Gunboats with Next Flotilla," *Jerusalem Post*, September 8, 2011, viewed January 15, 2011, <http:// www.jpost.com/DiplomacyAndPolitics/Article.aspx?id=237269>.

78. Menachem Gantz, "Jew-Hate Stems from Conflict," YNet News, December 3, 2011, viewed December 3, 2011, <http://www.ynet news.com/Ext/Comp/ArticleLayout/CdaArticlePrintPreview/1,25 06,L-4156355,00.html>.

79. m'Tsiyon Eliyahu, "Seventy Years Since the Arab Mufti Haj Amin el-Husseini," December 5, 2011, viewed December 15, 2011, <http:// ziontruth.blogspot.com/2011/11/seventy-years-since-arab-mufti -haj-amin.html>.

80. Chris McGreal, "EU Poll Sees Israel as Peace Threat," *The Guardian*, November 3, 2003, viewed on December 16, 2011, <http://www .guardian.co.uk/world/2003/nov/03/eu.israel>.

81. Nick Childs, "Israel, Iran Top 'Negative List,'" BBC News, March 6, 2007, viewed on March 15, 2012, <http://news.bbc.co.uk/2/hi/6421597.stm>.

82. Bruce Bawer, "After the Oslo Massacre, an Assault on Free Speech," *The Wall Street Journal*, February 7, 2012, viewed on February 7, 2012, <http://online.wsj.com/article/SB10001424052970204369404577206697 2422374842.html?fb_ref=wsj_share_FB&fb_source=profile_multiline>.

83. Maryam Namazie, "Racism, Cultural Relativism and Women's Rights," August 4, 2001, from a speech organized by the Action Committee on Women's Rights in Iran and Amnesty International's Women's Action Network, August 14, 2001, Toronto, Canada: "There are innumerable examples of its [cultural relativity] promotion in the heart of the secular West where different laws and customs apply to women who have fled Islam stricken societies. As a result of this racism, the veiling of girls becomes acceptable in the heart of Europe and men who kill women in the name of honour are given reduced sentences. The German government forcibly veils women asylum seekers it wants to deport to allow the Iranian embassy to prepare their travel documents. When a woman like Roya Mosayebi refuses to be veiled, she is beaten and forcibly veiled. When she complains to a German court, the court rules that the police acted in accordance with the law."

"Holland is another good example. In 1997, when the Dutch government wanted to deport 1300 Iranian asylum seekers back to Iran, it produced a report to justify the deportations, which made numerous assertions on women that reveal how far cultural relativists will go to deny women's rights. [The IFIR along with other progressive groups managed to push back the government's assault but its justifications are telling nonetheless.] On stoning the Dutch Foreign Ministry said: 'as at least four witnesses are required in order to prosecute for adultery, there are not in practice any actual prosecutions brought. We are not aware of any cases of stoning to death for adultery.' They further stated: 'while the legal and practical disabilities faced by women in Iran have been well documented, it is now clear that some change has been effected in recent years and that there are a number of signs that further and substantive improvements may be on the way.' They also said that: 'the presence of women is more visible on the streets than in surrounding Islamic countries,' and that 'While the dress code is mandatory, there are hardly any women voluntarily covering their face with a veil or wearing the traditional burqah . . . unlike Islamic countries such as Saudi Arabia.' On the fact that women have only temporary child custody they said: 'This system stems from Sharia law and is applicable in most Islamic countries.'" <http://maryamnamazie .com/articles/racism_cultural_rel.html>.

84. "Israel and Palestinian Timeline," BBC Online, viewed on January 16, 2012, <http://news.bbc.co.uk/hi/english/static/in_depth/world/2001 /israel_and_palestinians/timeline/1897.stm>.

85. Chaim Herzog, *Who Stands Accused?* (New York: Random House, 1978), p. 130.

86. Mitchell Bard, "The United Nations and Israel," Jewish Virtual Library, viewed on December 15, 2011, <http://www.jewishvirtuallibrary.org /jsource/UN/israel_un.html>.

87. <http://www.un.org/apps/news/story.asp?NewsID=19495>.

88. <http://www.jewishvirtuallibrary.org/jsource/UN/israel_un.html>.

89. <http://www.un.org/News/ossg/sg/stories/statments_full.asp?stat ID=4>.

90. Dennis Prager and Joseph Telushkin, *Why the Jews: The Reason for AntiSemitism* (New York: Simon & Schuster, 2003), p. 109.

91. <http://www.ajc.org/site/apps/nlnet/content3.aspx?b=846637&c=ij ITI2PHKoG&ct=875267>: "Some current manifestations of antisemitism in the Muslim world derive from the West. The so-called 'blood libel' story about Jews using non-Jewish blood for ritual purposes, which first surfaced in Europe in the twelfth century, receives considerable attention in the Muslim world. The government-supported Egyptian newspaper Al Ahram published a lengthy article in October 2000 entitled, 'A Jewish Matzah Made from Arab Blood.' In 1984, Syria's defense minister, Mustafa Tlass, published a book *The Matzah of Zion*, devoted to blood libel. In the 1991 session of the Commission on Human Rights, the Syrian representative repeated this ancient allegation by referring to the book."

92. Rebecca Leung, "Mind of the Suicide Bomber," CBS News/60 Minutes, February 11, 2009, viewed on January 16, 2011, <http://www.cbsnews .com/stories/2003/05/23/60minutes/main555344.shtml>.

93. <http://www.eumc.europa.eu/eumc/index.php>.
94. Juliana Geran Pilon, "Dr. Pilon Reviews 'The Abuse of Holocaust Memory: Distortions and Responses,'" The Institute of World Politics, August 11, 2010, viewed on January 15, 2012, <http://www.iwp.edu/news_publications/detail/dr-pilon-reviews-the-abuse-of-holocaust-memory-distortions-and-responses>.
95. Patrick Goodenough, "Israel Once Again Accused of 'Apartheid' at U.N. Racism Meeting," CNS News, September 23, 2011, viewed on December 16, 2011, <http://cnsnews.com/news/article/israel-once-again-accused-apartheid-un-racism-meeting>.
96. "Nadia Elia," The Palestine Freedom Project, viewed on February 14, 2012, <http://palestinefreedom.org/speakers/nada-elia>.
97. Susan Seligson, "Noam Chomsky Rails against Israel, Again," *BU Today*, March 3, 2010, viewed on February 14, 2012, <http://www.bu.edu/today/2010/noam-chomsky-rails-against-israel-again/>.
98. Israel Apartheid Week, viewed on February 14, 2012, <http://apartheidweek.org/>.
99. Gideon Shimoni, "Deconstructing Apartheid Accusations against Israel," Middle East Strategic Information, March 24, 2008, viewed on December 16, 2012, <http://www.mesi.org.uk/ViewArticle.aspx?ArticleId=106>.
100. JanSuzanne Krasner, "Stealth Jihad Invades Columbia University (Again)," *American Thinker*, October 10, 2011, viewed on December 16, 2011, <http://www.americanthinker.com/2011/10/stealth_jihad_invades_columbia_university_again.html>.
101. Ibid.
102. Eileen F. Toplansky, "American Jews and Israel," *American Thinker*, May 30, 2010, viewed January 15, 2012, <http://www.americanthinker.com/printpage/?url=http://www.americanthinker.com/2010/05/american_jews_and_israel.html>.
103. "University Officials Struggle to Explain Israeli Divestment Moves," The Investigative Project on Terrorism, February 13, 2009, viewed on December 16, 2011, <http://www.investigativeproject.org/997/university-officials-struggle-to-explain>.
104. Eve Spangler, Syllabus Human Rights and Social Justice in Israel/Palestine, fall, 2011, viewed February 14, 2012, <http://www.bc.edu/content/dam/files/schools/cas_sites/sociology/pdf/2012F/SC367Spangler.pdf>.
105. Matthew Fetzer, "Hate Crime in New York State, 2009 Annual Report," Criminal Justice Research Report, December 2010, viewed on December 15, 2011, <http://criminaljustice.state.ny.us/crimnet/ojsa/hate-crime-in-nys-2009-annual-report.pdf>.
106. Jamie Glazov, "The Campus War against Israel and the Jews: Joseph Massad," October 2, 2009, viewed on December 15, 2011, <http://frontpagemag.com/2009/10/02/the-campus-war-against-israel-and-the-jews-joseph-massad-by-discoverthenetworks-org/>.
107. Karen Farkas, "Kent State Professor Comes under Fire for Shouting 'Death to Israel' During Diplomat's Speech," *Cleveland Plain Dealer*, October 28, 2011, viewed on December 16, 2011, <http://

blog.cleveland.com/metro/2011/10/kent_state_professor_comes _und.html>.

108. Interview with Dr. Mitchell Bard, December 13, 2011.

109. Mitchell Bard, *The Arab Lobby: The Invisible Alliance That Undermines America's Interests in the Middle East* (New York: Harper, 2010), p. 323.

110. Ibid., p. 307.

111. Natan Nestel, "Groups That Demonize Israel Place Themselves Outside with Tent," Jweekly.com, January 3, 2012, viewed on March 23, 2012, <http://www.jweekly.com/article/full/63850/groups-that -demonize-israel-place-themselves-outside-the-tent/>.

112. "The Influence of New Israel Fund Organizations on the Goldstone Report, commissioned and translated by the 'Im Tirtzu' organization, http://imti.org.il/en," viewed on March 22, 2012, <http://israel behindthenews.com/library/pdfs/NIFGoldstone.pdf>.

113. Ibid.

114. "NPR Ignores Its Own Watchdog," FresnoZionism.org, June 2010, viewed on February 14, 2012, <http://fresnozionism.org/2010/06/>.

115. "Portrait of IHH," Intelligence and Terrorism Information Center, viewed on March 21, 2012, <http://www.terrorism-info.org.il/malam _multimedia/English/eng_n/html/hamas_e105.htm>.

116. Herb Keinon, "Israel: Fire UN Official over False Gaza Photo," *The Jerusalem Post*, March 16, 2012, viewed on March 22, 2012, <http:// www.jpost.com/DiplomacyAndPolitics/Article.aspx?id=262098>.

117. Herb Keinon, "No Sign UN Will Fire Worker Over Incendiary Tweet," *The Jerusalem Post*, March 20, 2012, viewed March 22, 2012, <http:// www.jpost.com/International/Article.aspx?id=262541>.

PART 2: HOW ISRAEL ARRIVED AT THE CROSSROAD

1. "Bibliography: Nazi Gold," National Archives, viewed on January 15, 2012, <http://www.archives.gov/research/holocaust/bibliographies /nazi-gold.html>.

2. Interview with Dr. Mitchell Bard, December 13, 2011.

3. Interview with Rafael Medoff, November 28, 2011.

4. "History of U.S. Immigration Laws—Historical Immigrant Admission Data: 1821 to 2006," Federation of American Immigration Reform, viewed on January 15, 2012, <http://www.fairus.org/site/Page Navigator/facts/research_us_laws/>.

5. "United States Policy toward Jewish Refugees, 1941-1952," United States Holocaust Memorial Museum, viewed on February 14, 2012, <http://www.ushmm.org/wlc/en/article.php?ModuleId=10007094>.

6. "The Holocaust," The Holocaust, Crimes, Heroes, and Villains, 2012-2014, viewed on February 14, 2012, <http://www.auschwitz.dk/docu /faq.htm>.

7. Rafael Medoff, "Golda Meir Sought Bombing of Auschwitz," The David S. Wyman Institute for Holocaust Studies, viewed on February 14, 2012, <www.wymaninstitute.org>.

8. David Wyman, *The Abandonment of the Jews* (New York: The New Press, 2007, reprint).

9.   Interview with Rafael Medoff, November 28, 2011.
10. "The only meaningful way to save the intended victims of Hitler's murder machine was to win the war as quickly as possible."(William J. Vanden Heuvel, "The Holocaust Was No Secret," *New York Times Magazine,* December 22, 1996, 31); "We have found some fundamentally new information about the president's views and policies before and during the Holocaust." (p. 4) "[W]e have uncovered some key episodes in changing American refugee polices previously overlooked. . . . President Roosevelt promised McDonald and George Warren, under the right circumstances, to ask Congress to appropriate $150 million to help resettle refugees in various parts of the world." (p. 335) (Richard Breitman, Barbara Stewart McDonald, and Severin Hochberg, eds., *Refugees and Rescue: The Diary and Papers of James G. McDonald 1935-1945* (Bloomington: Indiana University Press, 2009).
11. Interview with Rafael Medoff, November 28, 2011.
12. "The Perilous Fight: Anti-Semitism," PBS, viewed on March 15, 2012, <http://www.pbs.org/perilousfight/social/antisemitism/>
13. Rafael Medoff, "New U.S. Government Report Distorts America's Response to Holocaust," October 2005, viewed on November 29, 2011, <http://www.wymaninstitute.org/articles/2005-10-report.php>.
14. Interview with Rafael Medoff, November 28, 2011.
15. Abraham Ben Zvi, *From Truman to Obama: The Rise and Early Decline of American-Israeli Relations.*
16. "The United States and the Recognition of Israel: A Chronology," Harry S. Truman Museum and Library, compiled by Raymond H. Geselbracht from *Harry S. Truman and the Founding of Israel* by Michael T. Benson, viewed on December 16, 2011, <http://www.trumanlibrary.org/israel/palestin.htm>.
17. <http://www.trumanlibrary.org/israel/palestin.htm>.
18. Ibid.
19. Ibid.
20. Ibid.
21. Ibid.
22. Ibid.
23. Richard Holbrooke, "Washington's Battle over Israel's Birth," *Washington Post,* May 7, 2008, viewed on January 15, 2012, <http://www.washingtonpost.com/wp-dyn/content/article/2008/05/06/AR2008050602447.html>.
24. Clark Clifford and Richard Holbrooke, *Counsel to the President: A Memoir* (New York: Random House, 1991), pp. 20-24.
25. Interview with Dr. Mitchell Bard, December 13, 2011.
26. Mitchell Bard, "The Suez War of 1956," Jewish Virtual Library, viewed on December 18, 2011, <http://www.jewishvirtuallibrary.org/jsource/History/Suez_War.html>.
27. Howard Sachar, *A History of Israel: From the Rise of Zionism to Our Time* (New York: Alfred A. Knopf, 1998), p. 503.
28. "Speeches and Audio," The History Channel, viewed on February 9, 2012, <http://www.history.com/topics/dwight-d-eisenhower/audio#dwight-d-eisenhower-on-the-middle-east>.

29. <http://www.history.com/topics/dwight-d-eisenhower/audio #dwight-d-eisenhower-on-the-middle-east>.

30. Interview with Dr. Mitchell Bard, December 13, 2011.

31. Ibid.

32. "Charting a Difficult Course: Jordan in the 1950s," The Hashemite Kingdom of Jordan, viewed on January 16, 2012, <http://www.king hussein.gov.jo/his_periods1.html>.

33. Ephraim Kahana, *Historical Dictionary of Israeli Intelligence* (Lanham, MD: Scarecrow Press, 2006), p. 145.

34. Oriana Fallaci, *Interviews with History and Conversations with Power* (New York: Rizzoli, 2011), p. 58.

35. Abba Eban, *Abba Eban: An Autobiography* (New York: Random House, 1978).

36. Yitzhak Rabin, *The Rabin Memoirs* (Berkeley, CA: University of California Press, 1996), p. 106.

37. Richard Bordeaux Parker, *The Six-Day War: A Retrospective* (Gainesville, FL: University Press of Florida, 1996), p. xix.

38. Jay Cristol, "When Did the U.S. and Israel Become Allies? (Hint: Trick Question)," History News Network, July 9, 2002, viewed on December 16, 2011, <http://hnn.us/articles/751.html>.

39. Michael B. Oren, *Six Days of War: June 1967 and the Making of the Modern Middle East* (New York: Oxford University Press, 2002), pp. 36-37.

40. Rabin, *The Rabin Memoirs*, pp. 106-107.

41. "In June 1967, Jews from all over the World were electrified that the Wall was once again in our hands," Aish.com, viewed on February 10, 2012, <http://www.aish.com/jw/j/48964231.html>.

42. <http://www.aish.com/jw/j/48964231.html>.

43. President Johnson and J. William Fulbright (excerpt), 10:57 p.m., June 19, 1967, tape WH6706.01, citation #11908, LBJ recordings, CD track eight, viewed on March 21, 2012, <http://www.tau.ac.il/humanities /abraham/publications/johnson_israel.pdf>.

44. Benny Morris, *Righteous Victims: A History of the Zionist-Arab Conflict, 1881-1999* (London: John Murray, 2000), p. 362; *Airpower Journal*, winter 1989, viewed on February 10, 2012, <http://www.airpower.au.af .mil/airchronicles/apj/apj89/win89/hurley.html>.

45. Mitchell Bard, "Once again, Syria and Egypt attack. And yet again, only a miracle stops them," Aish.com, viewed on January 12, 2012, <http:// www.aish.com/jw/me/48893552.html>.

46. Henry Kissinger, *Years of Upheaval* (New York: Little Brown & Co., 1982), p. 496.

47. P. R. Kumaraswamy, ed., *Revisiting the Yom Kipper War* (New York: Frank Cass & Co., 2000), p. 1.

48. Abraham Rabinovich, *The Yom Kippur War: The Epic Encounter That Transformed the Middle East* (New York: Schocken Books, 2004), p. 487.

49. "The 1973 Yom Yippur War," ADL, 1999, viewed on January 12, 2012, <http://www.adl.org/israel/record/yomkippur.asp>.

50. Mitchell Bard, "Israeli Attack on Iraqi Reactor Offers History Lesson for Obama," March 16, 2010, viewed on December 16, 2011, <http://www

.britannica.com/blogs/2010/03/israeli-attack-on-iraqi-reactor-offers-history-lesson-for-obama/>.

51. Interview with Dr. Mitchell Bard, December 13, 2011.
52. "Operation Opera (Ofra)," F-16.net, viewed on December 16, 2011, <http://www.f-16.net/varia_article12.html>.
53. Agence France-Presse, "US Stunned by 1981 Israeli Strike on Iraq: UK files," *Hindustan Times,* December 30, 2011, viewed on December 30, 2011, <http://www.hindustantimes.com/world-news/Europe/US-stunned-by-1981-Israeli-strike-on-Iraq-UK-files/Article1-788961.aspx>.
54. Procon.org, viewed on February 14, 2012, <http://usiraq.procon.org/sourcefiles/UNSCR487.pdf>.
55. <http://www.fas.org/man/eprint/ford.pdf>.
56. Michael B. Oren, *Power, Faith, and Fantasy: America in the Middle East 1776 to the Present* (New York: W.W. Norton & Co, 2007), p. 575.
57. Ibid.
58. Tovah Lazaroff, "Netanyahu: 'PA Reneged on Central Oslo Tenet,'" *Jerusalem Post,* November 8, 2011, viewed on January 12, 2012, <http://www.jpost.com/DiplomacyAndPolitics/Article.aspx?id=244749>.

PART 3: A ROAD MAP FOR JEWISH VICTORY

1. Abba Eban, "The Saudi Text," *New York Times,* November 18, 1981, Section A, p. 31, viewed on February 14, 2012, <http://www.nytimes.com/1981/11/18/opinion/the-saudi-text.html>.
2. Thomas S. McCall, Th.D., "Palestine vs. Israel as the Name of the Holy Land," Zola Levitt Ministries, viewed on March 19, 2012, < http://www.levitt.com/essays/palestine>.
3. "The Temple," Jewish Virtual Library, viewed December 12, 2011, <http://www.jewishvirtuallibrary.org/jsource/Judaism/The_Temple.html>.
4. Rachel Ginsberg, "The World of Archeology Is Rocked by Evidence of King David's Palace Unearthed in Jerusalem," Aish.com, viewed February 14, 2012, <http://www.aish.com/h/9av/ht/48961251.html>.
5. Timothy P. Weber, "On the Road to Armageddon: How Evangelicals Became Israel's Best Friend," BeliefNet, 2004, viewed on February 8, 2012, <http://www.beliefnet.com/Faiths/Christianity/End-Times/On-The-Road-To-Armageddon.aspx>.
6. The Peel Commission Report, July 1937, viewed on March 16, 2012, <http://www.jewishvirtuallibrary.org/jsource/History/peel1.html>
7. David Meir-Levi, *Big Lies: Demolishing the Myths of the Propaganda War against Israel* (Los Angeles: Center for the Study of Popular Culture, 2005), p. 8.
8. Arlene Kushner, "UNRWA: Overview and Policy Critique," The Center for Near East Policy Research Ltd., November 2008, p. 3, <http://israelbehindthenews.com/library/pdfs/UNRWAOverviewAndCritique.pdf>.
9. Shira Schoenberg, "The Hebron Massacre of 1929," Jewish Virtual Library, viewed on February 5, 2012, <http://www.jewishvirtuallibrary.org/jsource/History/hebron29.html>.

10. "Grand Mufti Haj Amin al-Husseini," Palestine Facts, viewed on February 5, 2012, <http://www.palestinefacts.org/pf_mandate_grand _mufti.php>.

11. "Hajj Amin Al-Husayni: The Mufti of Jerusalem," United States Holocaust Memorial Museum, viewed on February 5, 2012, <http:// www.ushmm.org/wlc/en/article.php?ModuleId=10007665>.

12. Laurence E. Rothenberg and Abraham Bell, "Israel's Anti-Terror Fence: The World Court Case," *Jerusalem Viewpoints* no. 513, February 15, 2004, <http://www.jcpa.org/jl/vp513.htm>.

13. Yehuda Zvi Blum, *For Zion's Sake* (Toronto: Associated University Presses, 1987), p. 111.

14. The White House Office of the Press Secretary, May 19, 2011, viewed on February 5, 2012, <vhttp://www.whitehouse.gov/the-press-office /2011/05/19/remarks-president-middle-east-and-north-africa>.

15. "Speech by President at the Israel Forum Gala Dinner," William J. Clinton Presidential Center, January 7, 2001, viewed February 5, 2012, <http://archives.clintonpresidentialcenter.org/?u=010701-speech-by -president-at-the-israel-forum-gala-dinner.htm>.

16. Mark Twain, *The Unabridged Mark Twain, Volume 1* (Philadelphia: Running Press Books, 1997), p. 362.

17. Ibid., p. 349.

18. The Reverend Samuel Manning, *Those Holy Fields* (London, 1874), pp. 14-17. W. M. Thomson reiterated the Reverend Manning's observations: "How melancholy is this utter desolation! Not a house, not a trace of inhabitants, not even shepherds, seen everywhere else, appear to relieve the dull monotony. . . . Isaiah says that Sharon shall be wilderness, and the prediction has become a sad and impressive reality." Thomson, *The Land and the Book* (London: T. Nelsons & Sons, 1866), p. 506ff.

19. Anthony H. Cordesman, *The Israeli-Palestinian War: Escalating to Nowhere* (Westport, CT: Greenwood Publishing Group, 2005), p. 54.

20. Palestinian Central Bureau of Statistics; Israeli Central Bureau of Statistics.

21. "Terrorism in Israel," viewed January 12, 2012, <http://lindasog.com /public/terrorvictims.htm>.

22. U.N. Resolution 43, April 1, 1948, viewed February 14, 2012, <http:// daccess-dds-ny.un.org/doc/RESOLUTION/GEN/NR0/047/68/IMG /NR004768.pdf?OpenElement>.

23. United Nations Relief and Works Agency for Palestinian Refugees, viewed on February 14, 2012, <http://www.unrwa.org/>.

24. Yaakov Lappin, "Who Are the Terrorists Who Murdered the Fogel Family?" *Jerusalem Post*, April 17, 2011, viewed on January 5, 2012, <http://www.jpost.com/NationalNews/Article.aspx?id=216970>.

25. The Portland Trust Palestinian Economic Bulletin, no. 60, September 2011.

26. Robin Shulman, "Israelis to Quit Gaza Industrial Zone," *Washington Post*, June 9, 2004, viewed on February 14, 2012, <http://www .washingtonpost.com/wp-dyn/articles/A26259-2004Jun8.html>.

27. "Op-Ed: The Truth about Gaza," Israel National News, February 17, 2009, viewed on February 14, 2012, <http://www.israelnationalnews .com/Articles/Article.aspx/8587#.TwJThXORakk>.
28. Mark Twain, *The Complete Essays of Mark Twain* (New York: Doubleday, 1963), p. 249.

APPENDIX C

1. United Nations Security Council, Resolution 240, October 25, 1967, viewed on January 12, 2012, <http://daccess-dds-ny.un.org/doc /RESOLUTION/GEN/NR0/240/94/IMG/NR024094.pdf?OpenEle ment>.

INDEX